The Enneagram for Youth

Student Edition

The Enneagram for Youth

STUDENT EDITION

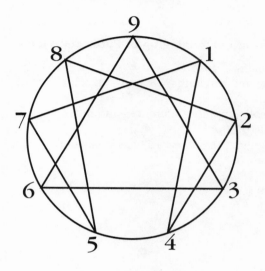

Rev. William J. Callahan, S.J.

A Campion Book

Loyola University Press
Chicago

Loyola University Press
3441 North Ashland Avenue
Chicago, Illinois 60657

Library of Congress Cataloging-in-Publication data

Callahan, William J., 1941-
   The enneagram for youth/William J. Callahan.— Student edition
      p.   cm.
   Includes bibliographical references and index.
   ISBN 0-8294-0730-8
   1. Enneagram.   2. Personality assessment of youth.   3.   Youth–
–Religious life.   I.   Title.
BF698.3.C34   1992
155.2'6—dc20   92–470
                                                                                   CIP

Ackowledgment

Cover and interior design by Jack Jasper

To the memory of Mr. Peter Swift Bird, whose
dedication to the youth of his people was an inspiration.

Contents

Foreword

My first acquaintance with the Enneagram of personality types was in a class taught by Robert Ochs, S.J., in Chicago back in the early seventies. He had just returned from the West Coast where he had learned the system from Claudio Naranjo, M.D. Naranjo, a physician schooled in psychoanalytic and Gestalt therapy traditions, had himself recently returned from South America where he and a group of therapists and educators had been introduced to the Enneagram by Oscar Ichazo. Ichazo ran an institute for growth and enlightenment in Chile, and the Enneagram was a part of his training program. Ichazo encountered the Enneagram in his travels throughout the Middle East, India, and Afghanistan where he met disciples of George Gurdjieff. The Enneagram was used for a somewhat different purpose by Gurdjieff, a Russian educator and esoteric writer, who was a contemporary of Freud.

Gurdjieff used the Enneagram symbol to explain personality types in a rudimentary way. Ichazo, more formally, brought the Enneagram to bear on the study of personality styles. Naranjo translated Ichazo's work into contemporary psychological categories, while Ochs brought the Enneagram into the Christian tradition.

So the Enneagram has undergone considerable elaboration and transformation. And this process is continuing.

When I intially learned the Enneagram, there was nothing written about it. It was passed on in the oral tradition from teacher to student. Ten years later when I wrote my dissertation on the Enneagram and researched its correlation with the contemporary personality typologies of Carl Jung and Theodore Millon, there was still nothing written about the Enneagram, and I was nearly reduced to putting telephone numbers and addresses for references in place of a bibliography.

Now, ten years later, there are more than a dozen books on the Enneagram and many dissertations completed and under way. Interest in the Enneagram has been remarkable. It is being taught worldwide: in Japan, Africa, India, China, England, Ireland, Australia, New Zealand, South, Central, and North America. The nine styles appear in all of these countries and cultures and also across age spans.

The system has been applied to personal and spiritual growth, to interpersonal relationships in couple counseling, and to team building in business, parish, and educational settings.

In this present volume, *The Enneagram for Youth*, Fr. Bill Callahan, S.J., introduces the Enneagram to an adolescent audience and their teachers and counselors. Since these nine styles are said to develop in childhood, they should be on their way to being fairly well established by adolescence. Hopefully the Enneagram will help young adults reflect on their values and motivations and behaviors to get a sense for the style they have been gifted with and have adapted.

Fr. Callahan is bringing his own innovations and interpretations to the study of the Enneagram system. He describes the nine types from his own understanding and experiences. He gives his theory of healthy and unhealthy development. He develops a description of each type's variation based on how it is influenced by the type on either side of it. He applies the Enneagram to an adolescent and early adult age group. And he spells out some implications the Enneagram descriptions have for spirituality, which he explains with some of the traditions of Native American spirituality; namely, the wisdom of the Lakota Sioux.

Although the Enneagram itself has been around longer than its youthful audience, it is nevertheless, like an adolescent, experiencing sudden growth and developmental spurts. These new additions need to be tried out in the experiential arena. Do they describe accurately the adolescent's varying experiences of himself and herself? Do they validly depict the paths of growth and deterioration? Do the suggestions for spiritual development prove helpful in the individual's life? The answers to these questions will only occur with time and use.

Fr. Callahan is adding his part in furthering the Enneagram system and developing its concepts. Hopefully he will bring greater clarification to his readers' understanding of themselves and help them augment their strengths and temper their weaknesses.

I believe the Enneagram has gained such widespread interest and acceptance because it so intuitively describes these nine realms of experience, these nine ways of being in the world. But like most things, it is appealing to some and not attractive to others. So we might take the advice of another spiritual sage, St. Ignatius Loyola, who suggested to his students and companions that if something is good and helpful, use it; if it isn't, then let it go. If you find the Enneagram explains your interests, values, motives, fears, and behavior, use it for yourself; if you don't find it particularly illuminating, then let it go. Perhaps some other system describes you better and makes more sense to you.

Finally, there is a uniqueness to each of us that no theory can capture. It is this essence or true self that this volume is intending to help us reach. If the Enneagram helps you get there, fine. What's important is not how you get there, but *that* you get there.

Jerome P. Wagner, Ph.D.
Loyola University
Chicago
February 1992

An Open Letter
to the Reader

Young friend:

You are about to become a pilgrim. A *pilgrim* is a person committed to a difficult journey to a mysterious and sacred place. This journey will continue throughout your life. The goal—the destination—is to find your goodness by becoming your own kind of person. No need to imitate anyone else; no need to model yourself after anyone.

This journey is discovering how you really are, taking charge of your life, making use of your strengths, and accepting your weaknesses and learning from them.

The energy that you will need will come from a deep and stubborn *faith* in the reality of your goodness, especially during those times when you can't see it or feel it.

The vehicle for this journey is *independence*. Independence is making your own decisions about how you will think, feel, and behave today. It is taking charge of your life to make your own kind of future.

Your protection is *wisdom*. Wisdom is understanding, accepting, and appreciating the beauty and truth about yourself and the world around you. It gives you the ability to make good judgments and good decisions.

The food you will need to live on is *compassion*. Compassion means to love yourself and others for all the goodness that is there and to forgive all the weaknesses and failures that are a real and unavoidable part of human living.

The air you will breathe is *hope*. Hope is the confident expectation that, despite all the obstacles in your way and all the twists and turns of the journey, you will come home to the goodness that is you and the goodness that fills all of life.

This journey is a circle. When you reach the sacred place you will find what you have been seeking. You will discover that what you have found you have had all along.

Take care on your journey, young friend. Have a good life.

Fr. Bill Callahan

Introduction

You can use this Enneagram to get a clearer idea of who you are and how you relate to others. It can help you to have a better understanding of your particular strengths and weaknesses—everyone has both. It can help you to discover the source of your personal power and how to use that power.

Using the Enneagram involves reflecting on your history and experiences, the advantages to pursuing a growth plan and the disadvantages of allowing yourself to slide toward unhealth. You must decide on your own. It can take some time to think about yourself and how you are—coming to realize your own special kind of goodness and beauty. It can take time to recognize that knowing and appreciating your goodness and beauty can be the source of great personal power for further growth.

The Enneagram encourages you to develop a plan for personal growth. It is not easy to develop an action plan, and it is sometimes even harder to talk yourself into doing it day after day. That's okay. Just work at it one day at a time.

Spirituality

I have included the description of each personality in a section on suggested spirituality. It is just a suggestion, something you might want to think about. Make up your own mind.

The first definition of *spirituality* I use is a way of perceiving, thinking, acting, and relating to both the material and nonmaterial world—a way of life. As such, the entire Enneagram approach is a study of "spirituality."

The second definition of spirituality fits the description of informal religion, a highly developed, community shared spirituality without a centralized, authoritatively mandated, universal set of dogmas, doctrines, or detailed code of conduct. This spirituality is, however, focused on a central sacred symbol and ritual.

I use the term *religion* to refer to a spirituality that has all the aspects that the informal religion has, and, in addition to sacred symbols and rituals, some form of authority structure to keep the spirituality and teachings on track.

The New Age spirituality that many people are becoming involved in is currently too fluid to define, but, as far as I can tell, it falls between the two definitions of spirituality. The word *spirituality* can give a person an uncomfortable, scary feeling. This is because very often it seems that preachers, ministers, and priests try make us feel guilty because of who we are and try to convince us that we are "not worth a damn."

Who needs this? Most of us already feel bad enough about ourselves. When I hear this I sometimes say to myself, "So I'm not perfect! I don't need you to remind me and rub it in." At other times I think, "Who do you think you are? You don't know me. You have no right to judge me. I'm doing the best I can with what I have."

This book is based on a spirituality of goodness. It doesn't "push" any particular religion. This spirituality believes that there is an invisible, mysterious reality and that within this reality we can find the source of power, the source of our goodness and beauty.

The spiritual suggestions I give are meant to help you, according to your personality, to keep doing the best you can and to do it wisely.

In using the Enneagram, I recommend that you refer to the suggested spirituality of your chosen personality type in the direction of growth.

Personality Identification

On the next page is a thumbnail sketch of each personality type that can be used as a tool for identification purposes. I ask you to pick one, and then turn to the description to see how it fits. If the type seems to fit, ask yourself why. If it doesn't, ask yourself why not. If the type you picked first doesn't fit, continue to "go shopping" until you are satisfied with a choice.

If you feel that you are getting confused, that's okay. Put this book down for awhile and do something else and come back to it later. This is not a test. There are no grades. Maybe a close friend who knows you well will be able to help you out. Seeking out a counselor who understands the Enneagram may be helpful too.

Some people choose one type and then weeks or months later change their minds. That's okay. A lot of times a person will at first pick the type "that I ought to be" or one "that I'd like to be" or the type "that others think that I am." Eventually, if you remain patient with yourself, one description will "grab" you, "hit you between the eyes." You'll get the "oh wow!" experience, and you'll know.

On the following pages are brief descriptions of each type. Each of the sketches addresses four questions that are answered differently by each personality type:
- What do I want most?
- What is most important to me?
- What is the worst thing that could happen to me?
- How do I see myself (on a good day)?

For example:

#1. THE JUDGE

- *I want to be morally right,* to improve myself so that no one will be able to say that I am not good.
- It is important to me that people behave as they should.
- The worst thing that could happen to me is that I become morally corrupt, a failure in my own eyes.
- I am a person with high principles—logical and orderly.

Please read through all the nine descriptions before you look for your type. After reading them, go back and try to spot your type—the way you are and the way you have been for a long time. When you pick one or two, look at the descriptions for each and see if they fit the way you are. Don't try to force yourself into fitting any particular one.

It's like trying on a pair of jeans. Find the one that fits you the best. Take your time. After you pick the one that seems to fit, it is sometimes a good idea to look at the others too—just to be sure.

There is a natural temptation to try to figure out other people's personalities in order to understand them or "psych them out." I'm sure that you wouldn't want people to do this to you, so I suggest that you just work on yourself for now. Okay?

Ready? Turn to the next page and begin.

Different Types
of Personalities

Choose the group of statements that best fits you most of the time when you are not overly tired or upset.

Pick One Only

#1. THE JUDGE

- *I want to be morally right,* to improve myself so that no one will be able to say that I am not good.
- It is important to me that people behave as they should.
- The worst thing that could happen to me is that I become morally corrupt, a failure in my own eyes.
- I am a person with high principles—logical and orderly.

#2. THE CARETAKER

- *I want to love and be loved,* to be helpful, and to be appreciated for what I do.
- It is important to me that others see me as loving and helpful.
- The worst thing that could happen to me would be to have to live with people who don't appreciate me or care about me.
- I am a warm, loving, and helpful person.

#3. THE PERFORMER

- *I want to be noticed,* to be admired for doing things well.
- It is important that others see me as being successful.
- The worst thing that could happen to me is that I fail at something and other people find out.
- I am self-confident, competitive, attractive, a winner.

#4. THE SYMBOL MAKER

- *I want to be understood* and to understand myself.
- It is important for me to find a meaning and a purpose in my life.
- The worst thing that could happen to me is for people to think that there is something emotionally wrong with me.
- I am thoughtful, sincere, sensitive, and emotionally intense.

#5. THE WATCHER

- *I want to know,* to understand everything around me.
- It is important to me that I see things clearly and correctly.
- The worst thing that could happen to me is that my ideas be wrong, incorrect.
- I am very perceptive and a person who sees things more clearly than others.

#6. THE DEFENDER

- *I want to belong,* to be safe in my own kind of friendly group.
- It is important to me that people be straight and fair with me.
- The worst thing that could happen to me is that someone I trust betrays me.
- I am strong-minded, friendly, and cautious.

#7. THE MATERIALIST

- *I want happiness,* excitement, to be happy, and to discover and do new things.
- It is important to me to always have a plan for what happens next. I always have a plan for the future.
- The worst thing that could happen to me would be to be bored and broke.
- I am friendly, fun-loving, and able to do well at whatever I choose to do.

#8. THE CHIEF

- *I want to be in control,* to lead, and to show that I am stronger than others.
- It is important to me that I be in control of what goes on around me.
- The worst thing that could happen to me is that things around me get out of control.
- I am different, independent, decisive, and respected.

#9. THE PEACEMAKER

- *I want peacefulness,* to keep things as they are (or as they were).
- It is important to me that everyone get along with each other.
- The worst thing that could happen to me is to have to say "no" to someone and have that person get mad at me.
- I am a person who is friendly and easygoing, but I can be very stubborn sometimes.

TYPE

the Judge

General Description

If you are truly a Judge, you most likely came from a very strict parental background in which your parents or guardians insisted that you follow perfectly the rules and duties they gave you. They would not treat you well unless you did this and, no matter how hard you tried, your efforts were seldom good enough. There was always room for improvement. "You can do better" was their usual response to your efforts to be good. You would respond by obediently trying to do better. If you were raised with your father at home, he was probably the stricter one.

As you got older, you probably took on adult responsibilities early. You may have had the responsibility to be a parent to your younger brothers and sisters. As a result, self-control is your focus. You are very hard on yourself. You have become your own very strict judge. When your fail in your own eyes, you feel very guilty. You punish yourself by telling yourself that you don't have the right to feel good; you have responsibilities. To enjoy yourself and have a good time is something you allow yourself only when you feel that you "deserve it." When you do let yourself have a good time, you still may feel uncomfortable about allowing it.

You are logical, systematic, and orderly. You are a hard worker and you take almost everything very seriously—"life is a serious business." As a result, whatever you do, you do very well, because no matter how well you do you always find fault with it and so you try harder. You are a perfectionist.

You are truly a person to be admired. You really, honestly want very much to do things right. It is good that you do the things that you know you ought to do. Wanting to be the best that you can be is a healthy goal. Many people don't seem to be able to be this way, and they mess up their lives and other people's lives too.

Justice and fairness are important to you as are tradition, religion, spirituality, and your culture. You understand the importance of rules, laws, and structure, and you are willing to conform to them. You also look to the future and like to be prepared for whatever comes.

You find it hard to relax your mind because if you listen closely to what is in your head, there is a supercritical voice always telling you that you are not good enough, that you should feel guilty, that you ought to be better and do better.

Sometimes you wish you could enjoy yourself more and act wild and crazy, but you judge this wish to be a temptation to be a lazy, pleasure-seeking, irresponsible, immoral person. You see that kind of person all around you, and it can make you angry.

If this type of person were not around, you wouldn't be tempted to throw away all that is right to become like them. You sometimes think that it isn't fair that they get away with behaving the way they do. They can do things that you can't.

If you notice, you do things because you feel you should do them, not necessarily because you want to do them. In fact, you are not sure what you really do want. You are only sure of what you ought to want.

You don't like to feel your feelings, your wants, your needs. They don't fit into the structured life you have set up for yourself. In friendships and love relationships you doubt your own goodness, and so you can be a very jealous and possessive person. You tend to not let your friend or loved one free to be with others because they might "dump" you for not being good enough for them.

You may not realize this, but you have a lot of anger inside of you, and sometimes it shows. You can be a harsh judge, crabby and unfair to others, without realizing it.

We all have feelings, wants, needs, and they are not orderly. They are not necessarily bad. If you try to bury them, they will just get stronger and stronger. If you let yourself feel your feelings and accept them as a normal and good part of life, they won't get too strong for you.

Some Advice

You tend to push yourself too hard. You probably want to loosen up a little, but it feels unnatural when you try. There are a lot of things that you can do that are okay, "innocent fun." Sports is a good example and so are many other school and church activities. You really need to do them. It is an important part of being a well-balanced person.

If you put yourself under too much pressure for too long, you can start to develop two lives: a life that everyone who knows you sees and admires, and a second part-time, secret life in which you do some of the things you believe you shouldn't do. In this second life you sneak out of the pressure cooker for a while, act like the people you have judged severely, and then return to the high pressure life.

Leading one life is complicated enough. If you also lead a second, secret life, it is only a matter of time before it will get out of hand, and it will surface into the open. Then you will feel really terrible about yourself. It's okay to be an ordinary human being with strengths and weaknesses, with needs and desires. It's okay to have a body. The body isn't bad. It's naturally good and beautiful. If you allow yourself to sip life's pleasures in your regular day-to-day life, you won't get so thirsty that you will get out of control and try to gulp it down.

The Two Paths

TOWARD HEALTH AND GROWTH

Work at accepting the world as it is and accepting people as they are (including yourself). Learn to be happy with a less-than-perfect world. A healthy One is a doer, and works to do his or her best—even though it is less than perfect—believing in the motto "if it's worth doing, it's worth doing poorly."

WARNING (Signs of trouble):

Crabbiness; sleeplessness; bad dreams; overwork; becoming emotionally uptight; thoughts and feelings that say "I must try harder and harder and do better and better"; abuse of alcohol, drugs, and sex to get away from the pressure.

TOWARD UNHEALTH AND BREAKDOWN

Self-righteousness; intolerance; inability to change your thinking (forgetting that there is usually more than one "right" way to live and do things); negative judgments of others; can't stand being proved wrong; doing the opposite of what you preach; punishing cruelty toward others; severe depression; and self-condemnation.

GROWTH STEPS

1. Do the very best you can, and be satisfied with that. Learn to relax and "sip" the good things of life, because it is a good way to be.
2. Become a good observer of the world that you can see, hear, smell, feel, taste, and touch, and learn all you can. Learn from your experiences. There are no mistakes, just learning opportunities.
3. Take the initiative. Become a leader—not a watcher or a negative judge. Since you don't have to do things perfectly, it's okay to start something and learn as you go.
4. Become a person who really cares about the feelings of others. Help them to become independent and strong. We all need to feel good about ourselves and about what we do. Help others to be this way too.
5. Pay more attention to how you are inside yourself. Get to know the goodness that is within you. Become your own best friend.

Now you can do what needs to be done without having to be perfect. Do good and worthwhile things because they are good and worth doing—not because you are trying to change the world to be as you think it should be. Don't worry. By being this way you will make things better.

Your Spirituality

You tend to be afraid of the idea of God. You are inclined to think that if God notices you, God will be as hard on you as you are on yourself—or even harder. You may also be turned off by your image of God because life seems so unfair. If God is in charge, then God must be unfair too.

This is your head talking to you. As has been said in many ways in this description, it is the way you think sometimes that makes life hard for you. Many people say, "I don't go to church. I feel bad about myself already; going to church will just make me feel worse!"

The only person who can make you feel bad about yourself is you. Since you are inclined to do this to yourself anyway, it is true that you don't need a spirituality or a religion that helps you to scratch that itch.

What will be good for you is to find a way to help other people to help themselves. Helping other people is a good spirituality if you have the right motives. The not so good motive is to help others in order to become a better person yourself. A much better motive is to help others because of their goodness.

Other people have a hard time seeing their goodness too. You can see the goodness in other people and then help them to see it themselves. Being with others in a way that you show them their goodness and letting them show you yours is a very good spirituality, a good way of life. Through this kind of relationship, you and others will come to discover the Source of all this goodness. The Source of goodness is not far away; it is within you and others. You feel it when you share it.

Fine Tuning

There are two types of Judges:

THE REFORMER

At your best, you have very clear, high principles. You see the world as a very disorderly place. This bothers you, and out of genuine concern you want to do something about it. You are a good student and a hard worker, but you have difficulty in relating to people because you always notice things about them that irritate you, and it shows. You tend to preach to them about how they should be. You have a hard time with the principle, "live and let live." You have expectations about how other people should be, and it is hard for you to understand how people can be the way they are.

It's good for you to realize that accepting how other people are is not the same thing as approving of the way they are. Being able to accept the way they are is just being realistic and practical. You can't fix a car until you accept the fact that it is broken and understand what is wrong with it. Holding your breath and stomping your feet because it won't run won't solve the problem. Anger doesn't fix anything; understanding and appreciating what is wrong will enable you to figure out what you can realistically, practically do about it—if anything. Some things can't be fixed. Some things just have to be lived with.

At your worst, you have a conflict within yourself. In some ways you are a disciplined, emotionally controlled person. In other ways you live in an emotional anger storm, and you can be irresponsible and unfair. You demand consistency (orderliness and conformity) from others, but you can be very inconsistent in dealing with them. Sometimes you are straightforward and fair, other times, because of your anger, you can be very hard on people, or take an "I don't care anymore" attitude. You are vulnerable to headaches, stomach problems, and other physical ailments.

Your anger and frustration come from nonacceptance of how people are, which blocks you from being able to notice what people are feeling. Most of the time feelings have a strong influence on how people think and behave. This is just as true for you, although you probably don't realize it.

Feelings need to be honored and dealt with gently in order for reasonableness to take control. Being able to do this for yourself as well as for others is called the practice of compassion. Being compassionate is not backtracking on your principles. Remember, you can't fix something until you understand and appreciate what is broken. In the same way, you can't make things better without compassion.

A final piece of wisdom: You can't change other people (they have to do it themselves when they are ready); the only person you can change is yourself. Reality is what reformers need to start with. Add compassion, and you will be able to do amazing and wonderful things.

The other type of Judge:

THE CRUSADER

At your best, you are a high-principled person who is very interested in helping other people. You are a people lover with high moral standards. You are generous and outgoing. For you, what is right and wrong is clear, but it is sometimes hard for you to understand why others don't see things as clearly as you do. You are also a very sensitive person. You feel your feelings more than your partner Judge does, and you have a better understanding of how feelings work in people.

You feel a personal responsibility for the welfare and happiness of others, and you do whatever you can to help. You tend to preach to others, but you don't mean to put them down. You are just trying to be helpful.

You are often frustrated with the way things are, and you have a lot of anger inside of you as a result. You are a kind and generous person, but when your frustrations get the better of you, your ordinarily good sense of humor shows its sharp edge, and you can overreact to others with anger and harshness.

At your worst, you know how to use other people's feelings to get them to do what you think they ought to do. You have clever ways to use other people's respect and love for you to get them to cooperate with you. You can make people feel guilty for not behaving the way you want them to behave.

You tend to tell yourself that it is okay to use other people's feelings because all you want is the best for them.

You need to be honest with yourself about being "clever for the other person's own good." You can get very upset if someone tells you that you tend to use other people's feelings for selfish reasons. When that happens, it's a good idea to check out for yourself what your real motivations are.

It is good for you to remember that underneath your helpfulness you are still basically a strict Judge. You have a strong belief that your way is the right and only way. You have difficulty with seeing that there can be many right ways to live, that people can have different values and a different understanding of what is important and what is not important.

To be really helpful to others you need to understand and appreciate what their values are and what they feel is important to them, and then help them, as best you can, to be the best that they can be within their understanding of life and the world. You have a strong tendency to try to make others become more like you. It would be better for both you and them if you could help them to grow in their own kind of goodness rather than in your way of being good. In doing things in this way you will be a genuinely helpful person and do your part in making the world a better place in which to live.

Some Final Advice

You are a very good and high-principled human being. The rest of the world needs you. You are good for all of us. Each personality has its own worldview. Each personality experiences the world in a different way. Every personality has its own special kind of goodness and shows it in its own way. Understanding and appreciating this fact will be of great value to you in judging yourself and others correctly. There are many ways to be a good human being. When you can judge in this way, your judging becomes less of an evaluation of others and becomes more of an appreciation of all the different kinds of goodness and beauty that is the very guts of this world.

TYPE

the Caretaker

General Description

If you are truly a Caretaker, you learned early that in order to get the love and attention you wanted and needed, you had to be helpful. By doing things around the house, by taking care of the younger ones, by running errands for your parents, you expected to be noticed, appreciated, praised, and loved.

When you were helpful, when you "performed" for them in the right way and they praised you, you felt loved, wanted, and needed. When you tried your best to be helpful and your efforts went unnoticed, you felt used, unappreciated, and angry.

Loving and helping others is your focus. Friendships are more important to you than anything else. Not just surface friendship, but real caring, sharing, lasting friendships. You work hard at being a good friend and adviser. You are a people lover. You make a very good friend, and you provide guidance and comfort to those in need. It is good for people to return the love you show them. You help them to become fuller human beings. Without people like you, the world is in very serious trouble. Don't stop loving and helping people— just include yourself as one of those people.

You tend to expect people to appreciate what you do for them. Not being appreciated makes you wonder if you are really a good person who is worth loving. When it seems to you that someone you care about is not appreciating you, it is as though they were telling you that they don't love you or care about you.

This, understandably, hurts your feelings and makes you angry at them. You want very much to be loved. You have a hard time loving yourself (because you don't see your good-ness), so you depend on others to make you feel worth loving.

You can become crabby and even mean to those who don't seem to appreciate you. Sometimes you find ways to make them feel guilty for not paying more attention to you: "Since you don't care about me when I'm good and helpful, then I'll be bad and get you upset. At least you'll pay attention to me then."

If you don't get the love and attention that you need at home, you will go elsewhere to get it. You know how to make yourself physically attractive to draw loving people to you. You will go along with what your friends are doing, and you will be very generous with them in order to keep their friendship.

The person you want to attract to you is the kind of person who will love you for who you are and treat you with respect. However, the kind of lover you attract is often more interested in having sex first—and maybe friendship later.

This disappoints you. You want sex to come after—long after—a deep and lasting friendship has been created. Since you automatically act in ways that you know a person finds attractive, you unconsciously bring this on yourself.

Sometimes you want to be loved so much that your imagi-nation runs away with you, and you let yourself believe that a person loves you in a deep and lasting way when the truth is that the person really doesn't. By doing this, you open yourself up to being deceived and misused.

At your best, you are a very caring, generous, and unselfish person. Without people like you, the world would be in very tough shape. Unfortunately, you can focus on others' needs so much that you don't notice your own needs. You tend to love and care for others much more than you love and care for yourself.

Without realizing it, you can become very lonely and not notice it. When this happens, you will see loneliness in other people and then reach out to them to care for them, but you are really seeing your loneliness in them. This can also happen when you are in love with someone. Like a movie projector in a theater, you tend to project your love onto them and think that the person loves you as much as you love that person.

At your worst, you can want attention so much, you can want to be loved and appreciated so much and be so angry at those you want to love you, that you let yourself get weak and sick so that the people you want to love you will be "forced" to love you. Some Caretakers even try half-hearted attempts at suicide to get the caring that they need so much.

Some Advice

The love that you need can't be given to you by someone else. No matter how much people love you and care for you it will never be enough; it will never satisfy your need. The person you really need to love you is you. You need to look at yourself in the mirror and love the person that you see reflected back to you. Very seriously, you need to really believe that you are a good and worthwhile and very lovable person on your own, whether other people appreciate you or not. The love you need is inside of you. You have a tremendous amount of love to give. Give that love to yourself first, and do for yourself all the things that you need to do to become an independent, self-reliant, "doing just fine on my own, thank you" kind of person.

Once you are able to do this for yourself, you will be able to be a great giver, helper, and caretaker for others who really need the love that you have to give.

The saying that "you can't take care of anyone else until you know how to take care of yourself first" is true.

The Two Paths

TOWARD HEALTH AND GROWTH

Work at becoming your own best friend and accepting the fact that love does not conquer all—that your helping and loving others cannot make them love you or make them change to be the way you want them to be. A healthy Two is an unselfish lover who does good things for others simply because good things are worth doing.

WARNING (Signs of trouble)

Trying too hard to prove that you are a loving, generous person; becoming overly friendly and pushy; feeling indispensable ("people can't do without me"); treating others as though they were helpless; feeling guilty for not being more helpful; blaming yourself for other people's problems; letting other people make you feel guilty.

TOWARD UNHEALTH AND BREAKDOWN

Self-pity; working on other people's minds and feelings so that they will become dependent on you, need you, pay attention to you, and praise you; anger and bitterness for not being appreciated; becoming physically sick so that others will take care of you; suicide attempts that might succeed by mistake.

GROWTH STEPS

1. Pay more attention to how you feel inside. Get to know the goodness that is within you. Become your own best friend.
2. Do what needs to be done to be a good friend to yourself. Do good and practical things for yourself that will make you an independent and strong person.
3. Take the time to notice all the love and beauty in the world. You tend to look so hard for love that you can't see that it is all around you.
4. Become a good observer of the world that you can see, hear, smell, feel, taste, and touch, and learn all you can about how the world works. Learn from your experiences too. There are no mistakes, just learning opportunities.
5. Take the initiative. Learn the best ways to be really helpful to those in real need, and then do it. Since you don't have to do things perfectly the first time, it's okay to start something and learn as you go.

Now you have become independent and strong. Help others to be this way too.

Your Spirituality

"It is better to give than to receive" is your kind of spirituality. All sorts of charitable, religious, social work, and health care organizations are staffed by people like you.

The difficulty with this kind of spirituality is that often Caretakers want to give goodness before they have come to know and experience the goodness within themselves. What happens is that spirituality becomes "I give in order to earn being loved" instead of "I know that I am loved by the greatest person of all, and I want to share this love with you."

Although Caretakers want very much to be loved, they usually have a hard time receiving love without "earning" it first. It is hard to experience the love of a person whom you are convinced doesn't love you. Your attitude blocks the experience of what is real. This can also be true in a person's relationship to God.

A way of praying that might help is to find, or form on your own, an image of the Higher Power that is different than the image you probably have of your parents. Find or form an image of a God as the gift-giver, caretaker; an image of someone who loved you first; an image of the God of Love who saw your goodness and loved you before you were born, before you had a chance to "earn" that love: "I'm good enough for God, so I'm good enough for me. God made me, and God doesn't make junk."

If you have not already done so in your life, take a chance. Form an image of a good and caring God. Believe in the possibility. Millions of people over the centuries have said that once they did this, their eyes were opened, and they came to know that what they believed was true.

Many spiritualities and religions have such an image of God, coming from long traditions of people's personal experiences of God. Many people call this experience discovering "the river of goodness" that comes from God, fills them, and then flows over into others.

Fine Tuning

There are two types of Caretakers:

THE DUTIFUL CARETAKER

You have a strict conscience that calls you to do your very best for others. People can make you feel guilty for not helping them more. You have a conflict between your feelings and your principles. You have strong likes and dislikes about the way people are, and you tend to feel guilty about not loving everybody all the time.

You try to treat others fairly and lovingly regardless of how you really feel about them. You tend to look down on some people because they don't think and act the way you feel they should. However, you try to keep your anger to yourself—but you can be rather preachy at times. You probably have a hard time admitting that you can be this way, and when you see it in yourself you put yourself down for having these "bad feelings."

Feelings are neither good nor bad. They just are, and they should not be kept stuffed inside you. If you can learn to accept people as they are and learn to live and let live, you won't be so tempted to gossip about them.

You have a tendency to try to control others and to make them feel guilty in order to make them live the way you want them to live. You can become very angry when they don't cooperate. You are this way not because you are mean but because you really care for others and you want them to be happy.

You shouldn't put yourself down for this. You just need to be very honest with yourself about the way you are as you continue to patiently try to help others—knowing that you can't change other people, knowing that you can't make people love you.

The other type of Caretaker:

THE PERFORMING CARETAKER

You are very friendly and outgoing, and you have many friends. You are easy to get along with, and you naturally attract people to you. You are very helpful to others, and you find it easy to laugh and cry with them. It is also very important to you that you be this way.

In your need to be loved, you have a tendency to sacrifice your principles to keep a love relationship working. You probably depend on other people too much, and so you tend to want them to become dependent on you, to always help them when they really need to become independent. You fear losing their love.

In your love relationships, you become very serious very fast, and you expect permanence and loyalty almost immediately. You need to slow down becoming emotionally attached to others.

Become an independent, self-reliant person and live on your own for a while before you settle down into a permanent love relationship. When you come to need people less you will be able to love them more.

Some Final Advice

What often happens to Caretakers who do not learn to love themselves and see their own goodness is that they can become very selfish ("me first") and mean-spirited. They can become arrogant and vain and end up punishing everyone around them—driving away those who love them. They sometimes start thinking bad things about themselves and start behaving in ways that will "prove" to themselves that they are not worth loving.

What can also happen is that the Caretaker can become a very clinging, complaining, possessive, helpless guilt pusher in an attempt to force people to love them and take care of them.

It happens not because a person wants to be this way. It happens because the Caretaker has not been able to make the leap of faith. They have not been able to jump off the cliff and plant their feet firmly in the air and believe in their own goodness and beauty.

The sad part is that this goodness and beauty has always been there. It was their original blessing from God. It is a goodness and beauty that cannot be destroyed—only covered up.

There are many, many people in this world who don't believe in their own goodness. Your great gift as a Caretaker is being able to help other people feel their own goodness.

You can do for others what nobody else can do for you. You can make them feel good about themselves; all you need to do is decide to feel good about yourself first, and then act that way. Once you do, you won't feel the need to prove it or have it proven to you, and you'll become very happy.

the *Performer*

General Description

If you are truly a Performer, as a child you received lots of attention and praise for showing off for your parents—doing very well the things that made them proud of you. By performing for them you received the appreciation and affection you needed. This made you feel very good about yourself, and so you came to need to be successful all the time. To fail at "looking good" would mean losing everything that was important to you.

Success is your focus. You are an attractive, hardworking, success-oriented person. You enjoy performing in front of people, and you appreciate the applause of others. You are also highly competitive. For you, success means standing out, doing better than others, and looking better than others. You enjoy being admired, and you will work hard to make it happen.

You know how other people wish you could be, and you are willing and able to be that way for them. At your best, when you strive to be yourself as you really are, you become an honest and genuinely admirable person. You can be a great example and an inspiration to others by showing them what any person is capable of becoming if they work hard.

You are a natural actor because you can make people see you the way you want them to see you. You can put on any role, behavior, or personality that will help you to achieve your goals. This means, at your worst—if you choose to do so—you can "fake it" very well. You can be a con artist if you want to—looking good for other people, pleasing them, and making them see you in a way that will make them do for you whatever you want them to do.

This ability to change your appearance can be a problem for you. You can use this power to show yourself as you really are as a result of sincerity and hard work, or you can take the shortcut and just appear to be the way you want to be. It is all a matter of integrity: being honest with yourself about who you really are and what you are trying to become; being honest with others and showing yourself to them as you really are.

A Performer with integrity will earn the praise of others. A Performer without integrity will deceive others to get their praise. At their worst, Performers become very arrogant and greedy. These people have little or no sense of themselves. They become tricksters. They want everything for themselves and will act in whatever way necessary to get what they want in order to become popular and admired by others. For them, goodness is a *surface* reality; it resides in cleverness, charm, and physical beauty. Appearance is more important than reality.

The Two Paths

TOWARD HEALTH AND GROWTH

Work at developing a strong sense of what is right and wrong; being honest, truthful, confident, responsible, loyal, and hardworking; showing yourself to others the way you really are (no acting). A healthy Three will do good things and do them very well so that he or she will be worth admiring.

WARNING (Signs of trouble)

Focusing on looking good and being very image conscious; needing to look beautiful and successful without having to do the work to make it real; arrogance; self-preoccupation; being a show-off; bragging; jealousy of others' success; wanting to stop other people from looking good; and gossiping in order to cause trouble for others.

TOWARD UNHEALTH AND BREAKDOWN

Extreme selfishness; compulsive lying; evil-intentioned behavior against others such as destroying other people's reputations, successes, and happiness and pretending to be "honorable" while doing it.

GROWTH STEPS

Become a good friend and a person of honesty and high moral values and behavior so that by being who you are and by doing what you do, you will be worthy of the love, admiration, and respect that you seek.

Make your own place in the sun rather than steal someone else's place. Do what you need to do to acquire the knowledge, skills, and experience you need to become the most efficient and competent person that you can be.

In doing this, you will find the success, happiness, and love that you seek. You will have self-respect, solid security, and, most importantly, your own strong identity.

Your Spirituality

Virtues are human qualities that make for good living. Your way of life, your spirituality, is most likely noticing the good human qualities that you admire in others and then living them yourself.

Any spirituality or religion will have some oral or written list of virtues. For example:

- Industriousness: being a productive, hard worker.
- Serenity: accepting yourself as being naturally a very good human being.
- Humility: seeing yourself as being no better, nor worse, than anyone else.
- Truthfulness: knowing the way you really are and presenting yourself only in this way.
- Equanimity: finding happiness in the present moment, being content with the way you and others are now, accepting reality as being good enough while not necessarily approving of everything.

- Generosity: sharing with others, in a caring and loving way, the goodness you possess.
- Courage: going beyond the feelings of fear; committing yourself to the long and difficult effort of doing what you know you need to do for self-development and growth in social responsibility.
- Sobriety: realizing that real happiness comes a little bit at a time, not all at once.
- Innocence: not wanting to hurt anyone, not expecting anyone to hurt you.
- Holiness: while sincerely working at leading a virtuous life, respectfully and peacefully living in the presence of a Mysterious Goodness that is more than anyone can see, understand, or appreciate.

This is not a complicated, difficult, or burdensome way of life if a person starts with faith: the firm and unprovable belief in the basic goodness of all.

Fine Tuning

There are two types of Performers:

THE LOVER

You have remarkable social skills, and popularity comes naturally to you. Your goals tend to center around successful human relationships. You are an independent person, so in your relationships you tend to want to be in control. You are also very selective in choosing those you want to be seen with.

At your best, you can be a very loving, caring, and helpful person. Because of the way you are, people fall in love with you easily and assume that you feel the same way about them.

It is important that you be honest about how committed you really are to them and what you want from your relationship. Otherwise an ugly situation could easily develop, and you could hurt someone whom you really don't want to hurt.

You tend to use relationships with people to make yourself look good, and you tend to play with their feelings in order to keep them. You can find yourself doing this without realizing that you are doing it.

At your worst, you can be a very jealous and possessive lover, ready, willing, and able to destroy what you want but can't have. The "vampire" feeds off the life of others and destroys them in the process. What can happen is that, not believing in your own basic goodness, you wrap around you whatever you see as being good and beautiful in the hope that it will "rub off" on you so that you will become good and beautiful too. The panicking lover will drain the goodness out of relationships until nothing is left, then move on to try to find goodness somewhere else.

All a lover really needs to do to find goodness and beauty is to look inside. It is there. Finding it inside, the person lets it out, lets it shine, and shares it with others. Through this sharing, the goodness and beauty just keeps growing and flowing.

The other type of Performer:

THE WORKAHOLIC

You are more quiet and serious-minded than your partner Performer. You are just as competitive and ambitious, and you wish to be noticed, but to prove yourself you focus on job performance and dedicated, hard work.

When you make mistakes, when you are disappointed or hurt, you tend to get angry with yourself more than with other people, but you bounce back pretty well because you are the eternal optimist.

At your best, you are very competent and a high achiever. You earn everything that you get as a result of your hard work. You may be tempted to cut corners to achieve success, but your integrity stops you.

You tend to work too hard and too long, and you tend to forget other important things in your life such as your relationships with those you love and who love you. You so identify your goodness with how well you succeed at what you do that you act as though you were fighting for your life in everything you do.

If Performers let themselves be this way, eventually they will put themselves under so much stress that they will do anything—

honest or dishonest, legal or illegal, moral or immoral—to be successful. In the process, they will, without realizing it, sacrifice everyone and everything that they love and value.

If they keep pushing themselves, they may ruin their health and become victims of "yuppie depression": become so stressed out that they won't even be able to get out of bed in the morning.

Some Final Advice

Performers can be terrific or terrifying people depending on how they define success for themselves.

If they put all their eggs in the one basket of achievement, their happiness and sense of worth is ultimately out of their hands.

Whether it be in school, sports, business, career advancement, or personal relationships, what other people do, how other people react to them, how the market plays, will to a great extent determine success or failure. It is not necessarily the best musicians who make it to the top. More often than not, it is the luckiest who succeed; they are in the right place at the right time catching the right person in a good mood.

If you are a success-oriented person, it may be a good idea to define success as doing your best at something worth doing. This way achievement comes to mean getting better every day, and success comes to mean never giving up. Who's your audience? Who's the one who knows how good and worthwhile you really are? You.

It is a good thing to have high goals for yourself. Goals are good motivations as you strive to do your best day after day. In this way of thinking, achieving goals is not success. This kind of achievement is like gravy on the potatoes. The real success is choosing to do something worth doing and working at it as best you can one day at a time. Doing this is truly admirable.

TYPE

the Symbol Maker

General Description

If you are truly a Symbol Maker, you are not close to either of your parents. From early childhood you've had feelings of being misunderstood by them and/or feelings of rejection or abandonment. Most children look at their parents or guardians as role models to follow. You didn't. You turned inward to your imagination and feelings instead. You have a sense of loss, of something missing, and you have a sadness within you that you are used to, a sadness that won't go away. In a way, you feel adrift in this world, an outsider. Sometimes you like this feeling, and sometimes you don't.

Self-awareness is your focus. Of all the personality types you are the most aware of what is going on inside of you. You may not understand what is going on, but it is very real to you. Most young people are self-conscious at times but for you it's different. You observe yourself almost all the time.

You can get "lost" inside your head, feeling your feelings or trying to figure things out. If and when you do so, you lose your self-confidence and you get confused, depressed, and maybe paranoid. You tend to constantly second-guess yourself, and this can lead to much unnecessary worry, insomnia, and self-pitying depression.

Because you are so self-aware and seem to be conscious of things that most people are not aware of, you feel very different from others. You work hard at being casual and spontaneous, and you wish that you could be this way naturally. You are very aware of the different masks you wear or roles you play throughout the day.

Because of your sensitivity to so many things, you sometimes wonder if you are not a little crazy. Relax, you are not. You want to be acceptable to others, and you love others deeply (when you finally trust them), but you resist being a member of any group.

Because you are so aware of your feelings you make a very good listener, and you are a better adviser than you realize. When you tell someone that you understand how they feel, you are probably speaking the truth—much more so than any other personality type who might say the same thing.

You want very much to relax and feel good. This makes you very vulnerable to all kinds of addictions. If you could relax your mind in a natural way the answers you seek will just come to you out of the dark, and you will be able to become genuinely spontaneous. In doing so, you will discover your goodness and your many talents.

You see yourself as being different from other people. You probably suspect that you are not as good as others. You also have a very hard time sorting through your feelings, and because your imagination seems so real to you, you can have trouble sorting out the difference between external and internal reality. You search for a special purpose in life or a special talent that will prove that you are good, worthwhile, important, and special. Depression, the inability to get yourself to do even the most ordinary things, and sleeplessness can be serious problems for you. You have very intense and gentle feelings, but you have a very hard time letting them show although you want to very much. You grieve over not being understood and over the insensitivity of the world, and you can easily slip into a fantasy world or into addiction in order to feel better.

Suicide attempts can be a way of trying to escape these feelings or to escape always watching yourself. These attempts can also be a way of punishing others for not understanding you.

You can be moody and overly sensitive, easily hurt, and fearful. Basically, you are in a search for yourself, for who you really are, but you are not sure that you will like what you may find.

You daydream a lot, imagining yourself as different kinds of people, imagining yourself doing wonderful things. Sometimes you just "space out." You can be very impractical and unproductive. When you are depressed, if you don't watch yourself, you can fall deeply into self-hatred. To avoid this, you need to do things that make you proud of yourself.

At your best, you are confident, friendly, cooperative, and very good at expressing yourself through talking, writing, painting, music, and other creative endeavors. You are some kind of artist; some kind of "symbol maker."

At your worst, you can be very irresponsible. You can get very down on yourself and on others, and you can easily abuse alcohol, drugs, and sex to escape your depression.

You don't pay attention to the rules of school, work, or the basic rules of life. Other people may think that you are rebellious. This is not really the case. Since you see yourself as an outsider, you tend to think that the rules simply don't apply to you.

Another way you may try to escape your feelings of confusion, worthlessness, and loneliness is to become a friend-seeker and an attention-getter through the way you dress and behave. In doing so, you try to create your goodness. You may also be prodding people to reject you—proving your worthlessness.

What makes you different from other personalities that act out is that you are not energized in doing this; it wears you out. What does energize you is in some way being able to express the way you really think and feel—honest and deep self-expression.

When you spontaneously let your self-expression just happen, when you stop watching yourself, second-guessing yourself, you surprise yourself. You discover what you really think and feel. You see who you really are. You discover your real talents. When you learn to depend on your own natural goodness and on letting it come out on its own, you will "find" yourself.

You love emotional intensity. Whether your feelings are happy or sad, you love to feel your feelings. At your best, because feelings are so important to you, you are able to feel the feelings of others. You can also, without realizing it, take in other people's feelings and think that they are your own feelings when they are really not. A feeling of anxiety may be yours or you may be taking it in from a person who is near you or from a person you are thinking about. It is important for you to learn the difference between your feelings and other people's feelings.

In a love relationship it is hard for you to know whether you are in love or in love with the feelings of love. If you are unable to stop watching yourself, you may emotionally shut down at the very times when you want most to let your feelings just happen.

Sometimes imagining being with a close friend or being in love is more satisfying to you than the reality. When you are actually with your friend or lover, you may feel bored, emotionally flat. You can be a good friend and lover, but not necessarily a loyal one. You tend to keep looking for the experience that will match your imagination.

You can be a very good friend if you can just trust in your own goodness. You can also be very hard to get along with because of your moodiness, your habit of putting yourself down, your oversensitivity, your lack of self-confidence, and your demands that the other person must understand you completely.

Fine Tuning

There are two very different types of Symbol Makers, and the advice for one type is not necessarily good for the other.

THE VERY PRIVATE SYMBOL MAKER

If you have a choice to be with others or to be by yourself, you usually choose to be by yourself. You are a quiet, gentle person and not very competitive or assertive. You prefer not to be noticed by others, and you prefer to let things happen than to make them happen.

You have a strong tendency toward spirituality. You look toward the unknown, the mysterious to fill the emptiness that you feel.

If you imagine your skull as being a cave and your eyes are the entrance to the cave, sit well inside the cave so that when you look out the entrance you see more of the inside than you do the outside. The world outside is pretty far away.

You are a lonely person, but you don't see yourself as such. You experience this loneliness as a general feeling of sadness: sadness in being the way you are but without the desire to be any different.

You are very attracted to anyone and anything that is beautiful, but when you reach out for it, it slips from your grasp. What you reached out for seems to be less beautiful than what you had imagined.

You are a shy person, and you have difficulty in relating to others. You are content to just be with others without having to make things happen. You are not the kind of person to reach out for advice and help because you don't believe that anyone can ever really understand you. This, however, is not true. Another Symbol Maker can understand you and appreciate you and how you are.

Move up closer to the entrance to your cave. Look for this kind of person. Go ahead, reach out. When you do, when you receive the understanding that you seek, you will feel much better about yourself, knowing that you are not really alone. Struggle to express yourself with this person; don't let your fear of rejection stop you. When you do express yourself you will be wonderfully amazed at the depth and richness that is your special kind of goodness.

The Spirituality of the Very Private Symbol Maker

The type of spirituality for you is a traditional spirituality/ religion that sees God as the Great Mystery and that humbly seeks a close relationship with this Mystery. No matter how much a spirituality or religion claims to know about God, we never come to know God through our intellect.

We live in a cloud of unknowing, but within this cloud we can come to experience and "see" the face of God and live. You are a mystic: a rare, much misunderstood, and much needed person. It's okay.

The other type of Symbol Maker:

THE PERFORMING SYMBOL MAKER

You are more outgoing, charming, and competitive than your quieter partner Symbol Maker. If you can imagine that your skull is a cave and that your eyes are the entrance to it, you live on the outside of the cave. You are very much aware of the reality of the cave, but you tend to be afraid of what is inside. It is quite a strain on you to live outside this cave.

You are a hyper person, and your anxiety shows. You are interested in spirituality, but at the same time you are also afraid of it. You act out your desire to be acceptable to others, but you often catch yourself trying too hard. You see yourself as an actor on a stage. You don't like the feeling, and you would rather just be yourself, but you are afraid that your real self, the self that you can somehow feel, will not be good enough to be accepted, so you go on pretending—knowing that you are pretending.

Since you feel yourself pretending and you don't like yourself this way, you are very vulnerable to all sorts of addictions. Getting high can become your way of freeing yourself from the tension that you feel. When you are high you feel more relaxed, and it seems easier to be the outgoing person that you want to be.

You really don't have to change the way that you present yourself to the outside world. There's nothing wrong with the way you are. This is what you really need to believe—there is nothing wrong with the way you really are.

You are too far away from your "cave." The further away you are from it the more uptight you will be. Slow down, pull back. Sit at the entrance to the cave looking out. Avoid alcohol, drugs, and fantasy-filled sex. All these things create illusions. What you want and need is the real thing. The more you can relax yourself and trust in your goodness the more your real self will come to you from deep within the cave. You will be very pleased with what comes. Trust in it.

The Spirituality of the Performing Symbol Maker

You have a deep need for a spirituality that puts meaning and purpose into your life. However, you will have a hard time finding a spirituality or religion that meets this need.

The best way for you to proceed is through the practice of *sitting meditation:* In this practice, you sit quietly with a straight back, close your eyes (or keep them slightly open), and try as best you can to let go of the thoughts that come into your head. It's like sitting by a fast-flowing stream watching the leaves and twigs come, noticing them, and then watching them go as they flow past your view. This way of praying is the art of letting thoughts, memories, and feelings come, and then letting them go.

At first, this practice will be boring for you, and you will be able to do it for only short periods of time. That's okay. This practice will stop being boring as you gradually let time stop and as you gather the confidence to let thoughts and feelings come and begin to notice what is going on inside your head and heart and letting it all go.

You will gradually find the effort to be very worthwhile. You will be calmer, more peaceful, and no longer depressed. You will find that through this practice you will become a very creative and highly productive "symbol maker." It will come to you in surprising artistic ways.

Through this process you will see the goodness that is inside of you come out before your eyes. When you appreciate this goodness you will know that what you produce is not really of your own making.

The goodness and beauty that you produce are really the images of The One You Seek: Images that come to you as a result of The One You Seek being with you and touching you. You will discover your own spirituality through the good things that you do.

The Two Paths

TOWARD HEALTH AND GROWTH

Work toward becoming confident, emotionally strong, spiritual, un–self-conscious, self-revealing, thoughtful, understanding, patient, sensitive, serious, and funny. A healthy Four will have great trust in the wisdom, creativity, and power of his or her unconscious mind and will find a way to become a promoter, defender, and revealer of the hidden beauty and goodness in the world.

WARNING (Signs of trouble)

Becoming wrapped up within oneself; moody; depressed; feeling not good enough; feeling different from others; paranoia; oversensitivity; self-pity; abuse of alcohol, drugs, and sex; becoming an unproductive dreamer; sleeplessness; avoidance of doing necessary things; fear of dreams; and fear of your unconscious mind.

TOWARD UNHEALTH AND BREAKDOWN

Deep depression that blocks you from doing what needs to be done in life; explosive anger; feelings of helplessness and hopelessness; self-hatred; self-punishment; addiction; and thoughts of suicide.

GROWTH STEPS

1. Do what needs to be done without having to be perfect. Do good and worthwhile things because they are good and worth doing—not because you are looking for perfection.
2. Do the very best you can and be satisfied with that. Get involved in "serious business." Keep working to do better simply because it is a good thing to do. Doing better is your goal, not perfection.
3. Become a good observer of the world that you can see, hear, smell, feel, taste, and touch, and learn all you can. Learn from your experiences. There are no mistakes, just learning opportunities.

4. Take the initiative. Become a leader—not a watcher or a follower. Since you don't have to do things perfectly, it's okay to start something, and learn as you go.
5. Become a loyal person who really cares about the happiness of others. Help them to become independent and strong. We all need to feel good about ourselves and about what we do. Help others to be this way. Defend those who need defending.

Now you can pay attention to how you are inside yourself. Get to know the goodness that is within you. Become your own best friend, and you will be able to express what is in you beautifully.

Some Final Advice

Don't concern yourself with being understood. Only a very few people ever really will understand you. When you live the spirituality that is yours, when you allow your real self to come to you, when you find a way to express it, what you express will be very much appreciated by others and helpful to them— and to you. Others will come to feel that you are in touch with things that are inside of them. Be to others the way you would like them to be to you. Your spirituality will keep you going.

TYPE

the Watcher

General Description

If you are truly a Watcher, privacy is very important to you. Of all personality types you want to be alone the most. You like it because when you had to relate to others—such as when you started school—you found it very hard to fit in. You may have been teased and picked on as a result. You found peace and safety by being by yourself, standing back and watching others from a distance.

You like to have time for yourself, to be with your own thoughts, so that you can pull yourself together and figure out how to handle all that is going on around you. You sometimes feel that you are being watched, and this makes you uncomfortable.

You find peace and safety by somehow hiding from everyone else either by burying yourself in books, television, working on cars, fixing radios, doing "busy work," or by finding a place that no one else knows about where you can be alone. When you started school, you preferred to keep "space" between you and your classmates; you were just more comfortable that way. You may have gotten into fights with others who wouldn't leave you alone.

You are loyal to your family, but you are your own person, and you don't get involved in family conflicts even though these conflicts bother you.

Thinking is your focus. You are a very private, quiet person, and you like to figure things out on your own. You tend to not pay much attention to your feelings. Your own feelings scare you—they're too "noisy" and forceful. You don't even pay all that much attention to your body. If you do notice it, it's as though your own body were outside of you, something that is "on" you. You have a good imagination; it's where you live. You are very much of a watcher of others, and you are curious about the things you see.

You like to figure things out in your head before you act. You use your imagination to practice relating to other people, then you do as you practiced. You are not always sure that you practiced right; you are not always sure that you really figured out the outside world accurately enough. It's very important to you that you figure things out right, because if you don't you might act in a way that will draw people's attention to you, and you might be laughed at or you might do things in the wrong way.

At your best, you figure things out very well. In fact, you've got things figured out better than most other people. They are the ones who mess up because they don't understand how things are. It makes you feel good to know better and to show the "cool" people how things really work.

When you are at your best, you appear to be the "cool" one who knows what's going on and how to deal with it. No one else knows how hard you worked to become this way; they don't realize how much time, watching, thought, and "practice" it took.

The way you come to feel your own feelings is to go over in your mind what went on after it happened. Through your memory and imagination you are able to experience things. It's okay to be this way. The important thing is to let yourself feel your feelings—even when those feelings are scary or painful. Let yourself feel them anyway. By doing this you will be able to figure out what other people are feeling by watching them and imagining how you have felt in the past. Once you are good at feeling your feelings and then figuring out other people's feelings, you will feel safer with other people and get along with them more easily.

At your worst, you get very confused about what is going on around you and you get scared, maybe even angry. You've always relied on your eyes, your memory, and your imagination to figure things out. When this doesn't seem to be working, you either withdraw from other people or you act impulsively without thinking.

When this starts happening you get very closed-minded and stubborn. Since it's important to you to have things figured out correctly, you start pretending that you do understand things when you really don't. You start looking down on other people for being dumb. You can become very crabby, even violent if people seem to be pushing you around.

What is happening is that your mind is moving much too fast. Your thinking keeps on going even when you don't want it to. You can't stop it. If you keep trying to figure things out all the time, your thinking starts going on automatic pilot.

Your head is full of thoughts that won't go away. You can start getting headaches. In this situation you can feel like you are going crazy. You can get into mindless activity, like watching one video movie after another or making or doing things without reason. Alcohol or drugs can be a problem for you if you use them as a way to go blank in order to pull the plug on your thinking—to make it stop.

This gets you into all sorts of trouble because you don't get around to taking care of ordinary day-to-day business or you get into trouble for what you did while you were "blank."

What is happening is that you are getting scared about not being in control. You begin to feel that you are in some kind of danger from the outside world. Your imagination can start running away with you—you can start thinking that something bad is out to get you.

Feelings of fear are causing this. Your feelings can create their own thoughts, sounds, and pictures. It can get to the point where you can't tell the difference between your imagination and reality.

Some Advice

What you need to do, even when you are at your best, is to stay in touch with your feelings, especially the fear-filled ones, and calm yourself by telling yourself that they are just feelings. You have good common sense. Use this common sense to talk to your feelings and calm them. When you are calm, you can handle things just fine. When your head starts speeding up, remember that you are probably getting scared of something, and tell yourself to slow down and just take a look at things for a while without trying to figure them out.

Just look. Just let the back of your head roll things around for awhile, and your common sense will bring things to your attention when the time is right. You tend to want to figure things out too fast. Take your time. It's better for you this way. You are a good watcher—so watch.

You are not as good of a listener. Learn to become a listener, too. Listen to other people's observations and advice. You don't have to "buy" right away what they have to say, but think about it. Remember that being a good listener is being a good watcher, too. Watch with your ears as well as with your eyes.

Another way that can help you to feel your feelings is through listening to music—the romantic, quietly emotional kind. Rather than "study" music, let the feelings of the music touch you inside. By doing this, you will discover and feel your own feelings, too.

Here's the hard part: Work up the courage to talk to someone about what is going on in your head. Try not to assume that no one will understand. When you talk with someone about these things, keep asking yourself what you feel about them. Be aware of how your body is talking to you. Start with, "I felt such and such when . . . ," and gradually work toward being able to say, "I feel this way now." You can do this by bringing your imagination up to the present, here-and-now moment. It may take you awhile to be able to say what you feel now, but take your time. It will come. Be patient with yourself.

Being able to do this kind of thing takes practice, and it's hard work. You will find that it is well worth your while because it will keep you from getting lost in your head.

If you find it too hard to do this in front of another person, get a spiral notebook and "talk to the book." Write down whatever comes, then take it with you when you go to talk to someone you trust. The idea is that once you get things out of your head so that you can look at them from a different angle, you can use your watching ability to figure things out.

What you might think is emptiness is really all the things that are inside that you are not in the habit of noticing because you focus on the outside world so much. What is inside of you is just as fascinating as what goes on outside of you. And you can learn just as much.

You might say to yourself that you are too lazy to do this, but it is really not laziness. It's fear. It's fear of what you might be feeling. It's fear of making a mistake. There's really no need to fear the unknown. Most of it is okay. The rest you can handle.

It is not your being right all the time that will link you to the rest of the human race. What will link you is learning from your mistakes. Mistakes are learning situations. It's how all of us human beings learn the most important things that we need to learn. Go ahead. Join the human race. It's an okay place to be.

The Two Paths

TOWARD HEALTH AND GROWTH

Work at becoming a very good observer of people and things. You have a great ability to concentrate, and you are able to figure out complicated things and are able to invent new things. Become well informed, practical, and productive. A healthy Five is very involved in outside reality and becomes a leader, an expert, in his or her special area.

WARNING (Signs of trouble)

Becoming "lost" in one's own thinking; letting your thoughts run away with you; becoming unable to change your way of thinking; becoming removed from the outside world; and becoming fearful, wild, and reckless.

TOWARD UNHEALTH AND BREAKDOWN

Because of the confusion that comes from loss of self-control, you isolate yourself from the outside world or plunge into it without thinking, becoming very fearful of the outside world and of one's own mind, becoming violent against self and others.

GROWTH STEPS

1. Take the initiative. Become a doer—not just a watcher or a follower. You don't have to understand things perfectly to act. It's okay to start something and learn as you go.
2. Become a person who really cares about the feelings of others. As best you can, share your feelings with others. Become a generous person.
3. Pay more attention to how you are inside yourself. Get to know the goodness that is within you. Become your own best friend.
4. Do what needs to be done without having to do it perfectly. Do good and worthwhile things because they are good and worth doing, not because you need to understand everything or to prove something.
5. Do the very best you can, and be satisfied with that. Keep working to do better simply because it is a good way to be. Better understanding is your goal, not complete and totally accurate knowledge.

Now you can be a good observer of the world that you can see, hear, smell, feel, taste, and touch. Learn all you can. Learn from your experiences. There are no mistakes, just learning opportunities.

Your Spirituality

The best spirituality for you is probably learning to do the exact opposite of what you do naturally. There is an ancient and very good spirituality that is based on learning to let go of the thoughts in your head and then just sitting and watching what happens in the nothingness.

As with Type Eight, the Chief, and Type Seven, the Materialist, the best way for you to proceed is through the practice of sitting meditation. This way of praying is the art of letting thoughts, memories, and feelings come and then letting them go.

You will gradually find the effort to be very worthwhile. You will be calmer, more peaceful, and no longer confused. You will find that through this practice you will become a very creative and highly productive doer. It will come to you in surprisingly creative ways.

Through this process you will come to see the goodness and wisdom that is inside of you come out before your eyes. When you come to see and appreciate this goodness and wisdom, you will come to know that what you produce is not really of your own making. It comes from Wisdom: something or someone much greater than any one of us that you are somehow in touch with.

Fine Tuning

There are two types of Watchers:

THE OUTGOING WATCHER

You are very interested in people, and you have a good sense of humor. You want to have friends to be with—not all the time, you like to keep to yourself—but a lot of the time. It takes you awhile to trust other people. You want it clear beforehand just what kind of people they are, what they expect of you, and what you are comfortable doing with them. Once you get these things settled, you do just fine. You can laugh and joke with them. Sometimes you surprise yourself by being able to talk on and on.

You make a very loyal friend, and you can be a very hard worker once you find out what you are good at. Once you get going, you are very good at what you do. If you are able to feel your feelings in the ways talked about earlier, you will be comfortable with others. If you don't work at feeling your feelings and learning from them, you will find yourself having great difficulty in relating to others. You will lose contact with their humanity as well as with your own.

If you let this happen, you can become very crabby and uncooperative with others, and you will want to stay away from people. If you let this happen, you will become fearful and alone, or you can become a follower of what others are doing and go along without thinking about what you are getting into.

The other type of Watcher:

THE INWARD WATCHER

You are a quieter person than your partner Watcher because you are not only a good watcher of what is going on around you, you find it easier to watch what is going on inside of you. Your feelings enter your mind when you come up with a good idea, when you figure something out that you have been working on for awhile. You are more comfortable with letting the back of your head tell you things without worrying about how these ideas come to you. By being this way, you can be a very creative person.

You are not as interested in people as the other type of Watcher. You can get very wrapped up in your thoughts because to you it is fun.

You are very proud of your ideas and what you can do with them. You take any criticism very personally. You can be hurt easily. When your feelings get hurt, you can get very angry and depressed. You tend to want to get into alcohol, drugs, or careless sex to escape these feelings.

It is important to not let yourself become afraid of getting hurt feelings. I know that this is easier said than done. When you have hurt feelings and get depressed, it seems like those feelings will never go away. They will. They will quiet down and even go away if you let them. Sometimes you don't want to feel anything, and at other times you don't want to let go of hurting memories and present hurts because at least you are feeling something.

Let them go. Let them all go. Don't "stuff" them—pushing them down deep inside of you so deep that you can't feel them. Let them come, and let them go. When you do, you allow feelings of your own goodness come up. You are not too sure of your own goodness. Your own goodness will come to you if you stop being so hard on yourself, and just let it happen.

Some Final Advice

For one reason or another, when you were younger no one reflected your goodness back to you so that you could see it, feel it, and believe it. It is this lack of trust in your own goodness that makes you distrust others—not what others have done to you in the past or what you think they might do to you now. This is the secret to yourself that you need to turn over in your mind. Your goodness has always been with you. You just didn't learn to notice it. It is there. Really.

TYPE

the Defender

General Description

If you are truly a Defender, you remember that as a little child you would get punished and not know why. You weren't sure how to behave because sometimes when you were minding your own business or doing something you did many times before without objections from your parents, suddenly, unexpectedly, you would be punished. What you could do, what you could get away with, depended on how the adults in your life were feeling at the time—whether they were having a good day or a bad day. You had to watch them carefully to see which it was. Sometimes it seemed like they were taking their own problems out on you. You learned to be always ready to duck out of the way at a moment's notice. You needed to feel safe with them, but you couldn't trust their moods.

Loyalty is important to you. You want to be a good friend. You want to be loyal to some person or group. You want to "take a side." You also value your freedom to trust people or not to trust them. You value your right to change your mind if you feel that they are turning unreliable or unpredictable—if it looks like they are not totally on your side. You also want to be independent, on your own, doing "your thing" without interference, but you want to be independent with friends.

When you see someone getting picked on by others you tend to get upset, and you will defend them. You know how it feels to be treated unfairly.

The virtue you value most is courage: Not Being Afraid. You like to test yourself to see how much courage you have. You like to test other people too, especially those in authority, to see if they'll stay friendly or get angry with you. You feel that if they'll accept you at your worst you will be able to trust them. Once you trust someone, you make the best friend anyone could have. (It's important to realize that courage is not being afraid of being afraid. Fear is a normal part of every person's life. Courage is not letting fear stop you.)

Unfortunately, you tend to test so much that even the very best people will get angry with you. Not many of us can handle always being suspected of being mean. Sooner or later you can make them act that way even though they don't want to.

Security for you is being acceptable to those who have power over you. However, you don't want to follow the party line because you have strong doubts that those in power are on your side. At your best, you will go along, trusting them. At your worst, "you can't make me" is your most common response.

You can be very friendly, loving, and charming when you want to get someone on your side. You also like to play antiauthority games: Sometimes you will do things simply because you know that you are not supposed to do them. You can become very angry and even mean when you feel that you are not being treated right.

When you get this way you tend to feel persecuted and think the worst of everybody and everything; you think that everyone is out to get you. You become angrily fearful, lose your self-confidence, feel small, get down on yourself, and act in crazy ways.

Some Advice

The world has both "good guys" and "bad guys," but, by and large, the world is neither for nor against you. It is not within your power to make living in the world easy and risk free. There will always be people who disagree with you, who want things done their way, and there are those who may be prejudiced against you. The world will become safe for you only when you do what you need to do to be able to take care of yourself on your own. This means that you need to be responsible, cooperate with the system to learn the skills, get the credentials, and accomplish what you need to accomplish in order to take care of yourself in the world as it is. Then you will be able to be your own authority and able to take care of yourself and defend yourself and others.

The Two Paths

TOWARD HEALTH AND GROWTH

Work at becoming cooperative because you decide to be so. In this way you will become self-directed, trusting, confident, independent, decisive, and trustworthy. A healthy Six becomes a wise person of authority and a person to look up to and imitate because he or she is a defender of the weak and the helpless.

WARNING (Signs of trouble)

Becoming indecisive; wanting to be told what to do while at the same time not taking direction or guidance from anyone; blaming others for the trouble you get into; becoming negative and suspicious; always thinking the worst of everybody and everything; and running away from responsibility.

TOWARD UNHEALTH AND BREAKDOWN

Becoming very hateful and violent toward all authority and toward anyone who tries to tell you what to do; becoming self-defeating; looking for trouble and causing it; blaming others for your problems; and becoming a "running rabbit"—often not even knowing what you are running from.

GROWTH STEPS

Put aside your fears and have faith in a world that will give you a fair chance if you let it. Trust in your own common sense, and obey it. Do what you know is the wise and courageous thing to do.

Become a doer of good things for yourself that will make you an independent, self-reliant, doing-just-fine-on-your-own kind of person, and breaking attachments to family, friends, and home until you can do this.

Once you do these things, you will be able to be a good example to others—a parent figure to those who need one. Once you become a good parent to yourself, you will be able to be a great example of what a human being can be.

Fine Tuning

There are two very different types of Defenders:

THE PLAYFUL DEFENDER

At your best you are very friendly, generous, cooperative, lighthearted, and fun to be with. People are naturally attracted to you. You have a good sense of humor, and you like to make people laugh. However, your humor often has a "bite" to it because you have a lot of anger inside, and it comes out that way. You are skillful at looking good in the presence of authority, but you don't like being told what to do by people in charge.

You are generally cooperative with authority as long as that authority remains friendly toward you. When demands are placed on you, you get grumpy and negative, and you will try to get out of the situation by not going to school or to work or by quitting the team. It's not that you are lazy—you are full of energy. You just don't like being told what to do.

You have high respect for your father or father substitute because no matter how he treated you, he would protect you from the outside world. You have a hard time getting yourself to do the things that you need to do in order to become independent and self-reliant. You want people to "make you."

You are somewhat afraid to become an adult, because you don't think that you will be able to handle the grown-up world.

When it seems that you are becoming successful at something you get nervous about it. You don't want to look too much like a success because you'll stand out and be noticed. This will make you open to attack and putdowns from others. You would rather stay within a friendly, noncompetitive group than stick out.

You don't like this about yourself, and you try to keep your fearfulness a secret. You cover this up by being playful and fun-loving although every once in a while your anger comes out and you can be destructive, finding some way to get back at the world for being against you.

What you need to realize is that your imagination amplifies the difficulties in the world. You can handle most anything if you just take it one step at a time, do the the best you can, and do it on time. You are naturally attuned to whatever might go wrong. Once you realize that what might go wrong is not the same thing as what will go wrong, you will do okay. The best defense is good preparation.

At your best you can get done what needs to be done. At your worst, you look for a way to escape the demands of growing up and to stay "just a kid" a little while longer. You are very vulnerable to all sorts of addictions. Drinking, drugs, and irresponsible sex are ways that you might use to escape the adult world. It won't work. Time goes by, you get older, and you'll find yourself in the adult world not being able to handle it. What you fear most will come true. People will have the right to put you down.

Your Spirituality

You are looking for a way of life, a set of rules, and a code of behavior that will make you feel strong and keep you safe. Most spiritualities and religions have these things. One of the things that religion and spirituality can do is describe a way, or ways, of living and preserve it for society for present and future generations. Look for a way of life that you admire and commit yourself to it.

The important thing to realize is that rules and codes of behavior won't help you if you see them as clothes you put on. You will need to look at the way of life carefully, see and understand the wisdom and virtues underneath the words, and then say to yourself, "I want to be this way. I will be this way."

Just going through the motions won't help you. You will need to really get into it.

The other type of Defender:

THE ANGRY REBEL

Unlike your partner Defender, you don't have a father or father substitute that you respect and admire. You wish you did, but you don't.

You are also quieter, more serious, more distrustful, and more angry than the playful Defender. You get into trouble more often. And when you have to face authority and answer for your behavior, you either keep a sullen silence or, if you've been drinking, you really tell them off.

At your best, you are clever and smart enough to cooperate and take care of self-development business without being noticed by those in authority. You "lay low in the bushes," and you cooperate with those in authority to keep them off your back.

At your worst, you put on a tough guy image to keep people from bothering you, although you really don't want to get into a fight. You like to "poke the sleeping bear" (authority), to hide and to watch its anger and confusion. You can become very intolerant and abusive toward anyone who doesn't look and act the way you think they should. You join with others who feel the same way. Instead of being a defender of the weak and vulnerable, you can become one of those who picks on them. You become a bully.

At your worst, you take an "us against the world" attitude, and you feel strength in being on the other side. You are also somewhat afraid of becoming an adult. You cover it up by being tough.

You can become an alcohol and/or drug abuser, letting all your anger at the world come out when you are drunk or high. You can then become very dangerous to others and to yourself. You may become self-defeating, causing your own failures, punishing yourself for not being the obedient person that you think you should be yet taking a kind of pride in your disobedience.

You won't seek out help for yourself; you are afraid to admit weakness. In ignoring advice and help, you hope that eventually everyone will "get off your back."

Although you value courage, if you let yourself get into the "born to lose, the world is against me" mentality and seek out other "born to lose" people to be your friends who will agree with you that it is not your fault that you are a failure, you will become what you most fear: a loser.

What holds you back in life is not other people; rather, what holds you back is your own fears of real or imaginary danger, of believing that, except for your close friends, the whole world is against you.

If you face the world seeing it as a dangerous enemy, it is very likely that it will react to you in a way that will prove your fears.

Your Spirituality

You tend not to trust anyone who tries to tell you what to do and how to live. This means that you will need to figure things out for yourself. You can do this because you are a good thinker and an observer of others. Look around you at the people you know. What did they do to make their lives harder and more complicated? What did they do to "wake the sleeping bear" and get it to pounce on them? Learn from their mistakes. Assume that what happened to them will happen to you if you do the same things. Become your own wise and strict authority. Learn from your own mistakes and the mistakes of others and become an example to younger people so that they don't get caught up in the grinder.

Some Final Advice

You have anxieties that don't seem to want to go away. Your imagination, like a movie camera, projects these anxieties onto the movie screen of the world. It is mostly your imagination that makes the world a fearful place in which to live. Life is hard, but that doesn't mean that you can't handle it.

Someday you will have a family of your own. Prepare for them. They will need you to be strong, wise, and skilled. They will need you to protect them and provide for them. Do what you need to do now so that when that time comes you will be ready. Your closest friends will be your future family.

The person that is most against you is yourself. If you have faith in yourself and in your own practical abilities and then take care of business, you will find that you have always been the kind of person that you want to be.

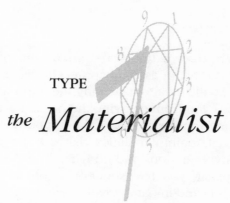

TYPE

the *Materialist*

General Description

If you are truly a Materialist, your family background is probably something that you would rather not think about. You may or may not have had a materially comfortable life, but there are painful feelings and memories that are a big part of that history. Your relationship with your mother is probably the source of this pain; thus when you do recall the family past you prefer to focus on your relationship with your father. If your father did not live with you or was absent a lot as you were growing up, you may have a longing for a wise father, and you keep looking for someone to fill his shoes.

Action is your focus. You are by nature an optimistic, enthusiastic, spontaneous, and outgoing person who really wants to enjoy life. At your best, you are a self-starter, a doer. You have wide-ranging talent, and you are not afraid to take risks. You are the person that gets things done, and you like to enjoy yourself as you do it. You like to be always on the go, and you enjoy making plans about what you want to do next. You get bored easily. You have a hard time staying with the here-and-now.

You are always planning ahead, and you tend to be more interested in the future than in the past or present. At your best, you "sip" life rather than "gulp" it. For every pleasant experience you have you are always aware of other pleasant experiences that you could enjoy—and so you plan to experience as many of them as you can. At your worst, you "gulp" life's pleasures trying to fill an inside emptiness.

At your best, you are very easy to live with. You enjoy, appreciate, and are grateful for all the goodness that you have in the present. Like a fine wine, enjoyment of life is in the tasting of it as it happens. You appreciate material things, and you are not at all shy about seeking the good life.

What keeps you from enjoying the present is that when you slow down and notice all that is there, you become aware of the unpleasant, painful realities that are also present. This often makes you anxious and uptight.

At your worst, you feel superior to others. You are very critical of others and impatient with them. When someone asks you to look at something serious, you are threatened and feel that you are being put down. Your spontaneous reaction to good things when feeling secure and comfortable turns into impulsiveness and anger when your self-perception of "having it all together" is challenged.

Ordinarily open-minded, you become very closed-minded and judgmental. At your best you can go with the flow of life in a lighthearted manner. At your worst, you become very demanding, picky, and get easily upset over little things. When things aren't going as you planned or when things happen that you don't approve of, you can be a rather nasty person and hard to live with.

Since you don't like being an unpleasant person and you don't like unpleasant things, you can become very flighty, flamboyant, and overly cheerful—acting happy and enthusiastic in order to make yourself feel this way. When you are acting out you can become a very annoying person.

You don't like being wrong. You have a strong tendency to rationalize: reinterpreting, arguing, and talking your way out of the weaknesses you have and out of the mistakes that you have made. You usually do this by blaming others or by trivializing: "It was no big deal anyway." You can pretend that things are okay when they are not.

Your great gift is that you can appreciate the good things in life; your greatest weakness is that you run from unpleasant, difficult, boring, and painful reality. You can be a very thoughtful and selfless person. You can also be very impulsive and self-centered. You have a hard time admitting the latter.

When things are going well, you are sensitive to other people's feelings. However, when you are into overdoing, overplanning, or overacting, you become insensitive to others, not because you are a mean person, but because you are preoccupied with your own plans, with doing things your way, with avoiding the usual anxieties and stresses of life.

You also tend to be very idealistic about how others should be; that is, the way others are is never quite good enough for you. This can make friendships and love relationships very difficult to maintain. Without realizing it, you can give your friends or lover the impression that they are lacking in some way.

Once you decide to stop liking or loving someone you seldom change your mind. This can leave the impression with those who know you that you don't need anybody and that your commitment to a relationship with someone is never really firm. It's as though you are saying: "I will be with you for as long as our relationship does not make me uncomfortable."

Since you are a very lovable person, this can put a good deal of stress on those who love you because they feel that they always have to be at their best. One mistake and the relationship could be over.

When you are forced to slow down, when there's nothing to do, you get very bored. Boredom is really an experience of anxiety and of stress. It is the feeling that things are closing in on you.

Slowing down, settling for less than the ideal, and facing the memories and feelings that make you uncomfortable are all things that you find difficult to do. However, if you do not do these things, the happy, pleasant life will always escape you. Things will never be good enough for you. You will always want more.

Some Advice

First of all, realize that you are naturally a delightful, wonderful, and fun person to be with—and very lovable. However, nothing comes easy, not even being your natural self. Here are some things that you need to do in order to be and to stay the wonderful person you naturally are.

Learn how to face the painful issues in your life by calmly letting them come to you without thinking them away through rationalization or trivialization. Doing this will be difficult for you. You may feel awful and depressed for a while, but this painful feeling won't last forever even though it seems that it will.

You have a habit of running ahead of your problems. Stop. Let them come, sit with them, accept the realities that they contain, learn from them, and then let them go. You can't let something go until you hold it in your hand. If you hold it, look at it, feel it, understand it, and then let it go, it won't come back.

See each problem as a summer storm. You can't outrun it, so let it come and rain on you. The storm won't stay. It will move on and the air will be cleaner and fresher. The day will be brighter than ever before.

By doing this you will increase your own personal depth and be able to appreciate the simpler, more ordinary things in life. You will become a more sensitive, more loving, and more lovable person.

A strong fear of yours is that if you face the thunder in your life you will discover that you are not a very good person. The truth is that if you do this, you will discover that you are actually a better person than you think you are. You will discover your natural goodness: the goodness that everyone else has always been able to see in you (except, maybe, your mother).

When you lose your temper, count to ten and put yourself in a quiet place. Notice that you tend to see people and situations in black and white, all good or all bad. Notice that when you need to explain yourself to someone, you tend to make up a story to avoid painful embarrassment.

Eating humble pie is not easy for you to do. It's okay to admit your mistakes and weaknesses. It's a very humanizing thing to do.

Join the human race; you'll be in good company. Be alert to your impulsive nature. Learn to think twice before you act. Think of the consequences before you go ahead.

Listen to the advice that is given you. You really don't have all the answers—neither does anyone else. Be a giver, not a taker. Your hidden, special gift is being grateful for the simple, ordinary things in life. Once you become an appreciator, you will be able to be a giver too. Then you won't find yourself always planning a better future. Happiness is discovering the goodness in the present.

You need to stay away from drugs that pick you up and make you feel better. Once you start, it will be very hard to stop. The best high that you can have is facing the pain that self-honesty can bring and then seeing how wonderful you really are.

Learn to live in the present and appreciate all the goodness that is there. By really getting into the here and now, you will discover how much you have been missing. You will probably discover that what you have been looking for you already have.

Don't be afraid to let people get close to you. Once you join the human race, accept people as they are, and love the ones you're with, your judgmentalism won't ruin the love you have found. You can be independent and deeply involved in a committed love relationship too. You really don't want to be alone even though you have a hard time admitting this.

The Two Paths

TOWARD HEALTH AND GROWTH

Work to become happy, relaxed, and appreciative of the good things in the present. You will then be able to be responsible, productive, enthusiastic, and able to do many things well. A healthy Seven is a very likeable doer who thinks before he or she acts, looking to the consequences of actions before acting.

WARNING (Signs of trouble)

Becoming a person who has to be in constant motion, having fun all the time; getting into trouble as a result of not thinking before doing; running from doing any serious thinking about one's self and about life; running from the consequences of one's own behavior; blaming others when things go wrong;

becoming demanding; being insensitive to other people's feelings; becoming unable to take advice or correction; abusing alcohol, drugs, and sex; and getting high on activity.

TOWARD UNHEALTH AND BREAKDOWN

You are in trouble when you become reckless and out of control, when you panic at the confusion you feel, when you go into constant motion, when you become overly enthusiastic and cheerful, and when you become picky, angry, and judgmental.

GROWTH STEPS

1. Slow down. Appreciate the world that you can see, hear, smell, feel, taste, and touch, and learn all you can. Learn from your experiences. Happiness is found in noticing the simple and ordinary things in life, not in only doing new and exciting things.
2. Take the initiative. Become a doer of important, worthwhile things—not a complainer. You will find the satisfaction you seek by doing worthwhile things well. Think first, and learn as you go.
3. Become a person who really cares about the feelings of others. Help them to appreciate life too. We all need to be excited about the world and about what we do. Help others to be this way too.
4. Pay more attention to how you are inside. Get to know the pain and goodness that is within you. Happiness is hidden inside of you.
5. Do what needs to be done without needing to have fun. Do good and worthwhile things because they are good and worth doing—not because they are exciting.

Now you can really enjoy life and be satisfied with it. Living will no longer be boring or unpleasant simply because now you can appreciate the goodness that is everywhere. Doing good things well is your goal. Happiness will find you.

Your Spirituality

There are many kinds of spirituality and many different ways of praying. Whatever your preference, there is a way of meditation that would be very good for you—but it is also very hard.

As with Type Five, the Watcher, and Type Eight, the Chief, the practice of sitting meditation may also help you. In this practice, you sit quietly with a straight back, close your eyes (or keep them slightly open), and try as best you can to let go of the thoughts that come into your head. It's like sitting by a fast-flowing stream watching the leaves and twigs come, noticing them, and then watching them go as they flow past your view. This way of praying is the art of letting thoughts, memories, and feelings come, and then letting them go.

You will gradually find the effort to be very worthwhile. You will be calmer and more peaceful. You will find that you will be able to appreciate the goodness of the present much more than before.

Fine Tuning

There are two types of Materialists:

THE PERSON-ORIENTED MATERIALIST

There are two sides to you that don't always work well together. One side finds security in having the approval of other people. The other side makes you able to take care of yourself whether people approve of you or not. To solve this tension you don't have to choose one or the other. The best way is to go ahead and take care of yourself, and then find people who will love and support you as you are.

If you look for the approval of others first, if you look for someone to take care of you, your life will be hard. You will fall in and out of love often because no love relationship will be able to meet that need. After the fun-filled rush of love is over you will become bored and disappointed, and you will impulsively move on to another love.

You will probably become anxious about having enough money, become very demanding of others, and grow indecisive and confused.

At worst, you will become helpless and pitiful, demanding that other people take care of you. You will become angry and drive them away and then go after them again. You may even become impulsively self-destructive and suicidal.

The other type of Materialist:

THE AGGRESSIVE MATERIALIST

You are a very forceful go-getter. No one stands in your way, and you get what you want. You are more enthusiastic than your partner Materialist, and you are more self-confident. You have the ability to be a very good leader. You go after what you want, and you won't stop until you get it.

However, your single-mindedness can be at the cost of the wants, needs, and ambitions of the people who love you. Your partner Materialist prefers to avoid conflicts, but you don't. Your impulse is to confront and conquer.

At your worst, you may even ignore the principles of right and wrong and become ruthless. When angry, you can become physical and attack those who appear to challenge you.

Some Final Advice

The continuing fact of life for you is that you will have difficulty finding satisfaction with your life and your love relationships. You have trouble getting below the surface of human experience. This is what causes your dissatisfaction.

Learn to look around in the present moment, and be grateful for what you have and for what you do. Happiness does not come to you from the outside world; it comes to you from the world inside of you.

TYPE

the Chief

General Description

If you are truly a Chief, you may have grown up in a family in which to survive you felt that you had to be very strong-minded and forceful to keep others in their place so that they could not dominate you. You felt that if you did not "face them down," they would "stomp all over you." Many people would like to believe that they are fearless, but they pretend a lot. You don't pretend; you *are* fearless.

Power to control is your focus. It is your greatest strength. It is very important to you that you be in charge of the world around you. You are the true rugged individualist: self-reliant, self-confident, self-starting, and aggressive. You control through the power of your strong-willed personality more than through physical force. You don't have to use physical force. In a "stare-down," the other person will back off. Only when you have to face another Chief will you have to "take care of business" in a physical way. Even then you seldom do because of your respect for another Chief. You'll usually work out some kind of an arrangement that you both can live with, not because you fear each other but because you respect each other.

You enjoy taking on challenges because you enjoy using the power of your personality and watching it "work its wonders."

Honor and courage are important to you. You have a tremendous amount of energy and goodwill. People naturally look to you for leadership because you are an outgoing, take-charge person, and a good organizer. At your best, you are sensitive to the needs of people who can be pushed around. You become their protector. You would like to see people taking care of themselves, and you genuinely care for those who are trying but who need help from time to time.

Because your personality is so forceful you tend to be a pushy person, testing other people's strength when it is not necessary. You tend to take charge even when things are going along just fine without your leadership. As a result, you tend to take power from people rather than empower them.

At your worst, you judge others harshly for being weak-minded and cowardly. When you feel that you are being criticized, you become angry and instinctively take a face-off stance. You develop an exaggerated sense of your own power and importance and force yourself on others.

You are good at organizing and leading and when you are in a new situation or when things aren't going your way, you can become very angry, aggressive, revengeful, and unfair. You turn into a bully. You pout, and your love and concern for people turns into a love and concern only for yourself.

Although you prefer not to use physical force (you don't have to), the exercise of your power to dominate those around you is a very physical experience for you. Your feeling of power is a very pleasant physical feeling.

This feeling can flow over into your love relationships. If you are not careful, you can act like a lion dominating his mate. However, the only mate that you respect is one who can stop you cold in your tracks.

When you become filled with yourself, you feel that you can "push back the flood waters." In the process of forcing yourself on others, you change from being a big-hearted leader and turn into an oppressive, violent dictator, taking revenge against anyone who might challenge your absolute authority. The number of your enemies grows day by day, and you begin to experience something that you never experienced before—fear.

You will feel your power draining, begin to feel weak and helpless and become paranoid and violent. Once you were concerned about the welfare and happiness of others. Things have changed. There is only one person in your life that needs protection—you. You push people out in front of you to protect yourself.

You end up hiding in a fortress being attacked by all the "little people" you once controlled with an iron fist. You can no longer hold back the flood waters, and the one thing that you always wanted to avoid, the one thing that you were so good at preventing, happens. You are overwhelmed.

Some Advice

You have a powerful personality that is like a two-edged sword. Your happiness and security depend on how you use it.

You can be a tremendous force for good if you can remember to be an ordinary member of the human race—a gifted person among equals. Every personality has a special gift; you are not the only one that is gifted. Learn to see the gifts that other people have. Some have the gift of wisdom; you need that. Others have the gift of compassion; you need that too. Some people were never meant to be leaders, but they can be very loyal friends who will "protect your back" if you are good to them. If you are not good to them, they can become your hidden enemies.

There are no "little people," just other kinds of people. You can become and remain "king of the mountain" only if the mountain lets you be king. Mountains can blow their tops.

What will make and keep you an active Chief is kindness. Power and kindness is an unbeatable combination. On the other hand, power and arrogance is a combination that is destructive; ultimately, self-destructive. This is why a Spirituality of Kindness is so necessary for you.

The Two Paths

TOWARD HEALTH AND GROWTH

Work at becoming a generous, big-hearted person, self-controlled, courageous, confident, a natural leader, and an inspiration to others. A healthy Eight becomes an honorable protector of the people, helping them to grow independent and strong.

WARNING (Signs of trouble)

Becoming arrogant; needing to always be in charge; needing to be in situations where you can order others around; being overly assertive; looking for enemies—and making them—and feeling the need to payback when you really don't have to.

TOWARD UNHEALTH AND BREAKDOWN

Owing to the fear of not being in control of those around them, Chiefs become unable to take any advice. They become very paranoid, fearing that others are trying to destroy them. They become bullies and eventually ruthless dictators seeking revenge against real and imagined enemies (anyone who does not conform to their wishes). They will do anything that they feel they need to do to stay on top.

GROWTH STEPS

1. Become a person who really cares about the feelings of others. Help them to become independent and strong. This is the way you are. Help others to be this way, too.
2. Pay more attention to how you are inside yourself. Get to know and love the gentle person that is within you. Doing this will help you to become and remain a full member of the human race.
3. Do the very best you can, and be satisfied with that. Keep working to do better simply because it is a good way to be. Doing good things with others is your goal, not ruling over others.
4. Do good and worthwhile things with others. Do things with others because they have valuable gifts too—gifts that you do not have.
5. Become a good observer of all the kindness and beauty that is so very much a part of our world. Learn to feel this goodness. Learn from your experiences. There are no mistakes, just learning opportunities.

Now you can become a leader—not a dictator. Since you have learned to be with and care for others, you can be the person in charge.

Your Spirituality

Spirituality is recognizing your place in the world and then relating to everything else from this personal center. If you misjudge your place, nothing will work out for you, and your life will be an aimless wandering.

Secretly, deep down in your gut, you want to be blindly loyal to someone, you want to be sheltered, protected, and cared for by someone whom you can trust absolutely. You really don't want to always have to be on constant alert and always in charge.

Your power is not something that you created yourself. You didn't make it; you found it in your pocket. Where did it come from? Why was it given to you? Can it be taken back if you don't use it right?

You need to be in touch with the Source of your power, your Higher Power—God; otherwise, you'll move beyond your source of supply and find that you are cut off and isolated.

This Source is not something that you can see and check out. You can only feel it. When you feel your power, you are experiencing the special gift that God has given you. To use it properly you need to get to know the Source, and respect it.

One method that many Chiefs have used over the centuries to be in touch with the Source is through meditation or sitting meditation. In this practice, you sit quietly with a straight back, close your eyes (or keep them slightly open), and try as best as you can to let go of the thoughts that come into your head. It's like sitting by a fast-flowing stream watching the leaves and twigs come, noticing them, and then watching them go as they flow past your view.

This way of praying—which also applies to Types Four (Symbol Maker), Five (Watcher), and Seven (Materialist)—is the art of letting thoughts, memories, and feelings come and then letting them go.

At first, this will be boring for you, and you will be able to do it for only short periods of time. That's okay. It will cease to be boring as you gradually let time stop and as you gather the confidence to let thoughts and feelings come and begin to notice what is going on inside your head and heart, and letting it all go.

Some people who do this try to avoid the thoughts and feelings that come to them. This is a mistake. You tend to want to be in control of things. You will need to work at just letting things happen.

You have a lot of anger in you that you may not be aware of. Let it come, then let it drift away like smoke from a fire. Let the energy from your gut rise up through your body and fill your chest, and then breathe it out. This may seem a strange thing to do, but if you do it, your anger, your power, your body energy will turn into heart energy, and you will become a kinder, gentler person. Then let the energy rise up in your throat, and fill your head. This can be a very powerful spiritual experience. Through it you may come to know where your power comes from.

Fine Tuning

There are two types of Chiefs:

THE THRILL-SEEKER

You are the most aggressive and independent of all personality types. You are very outgoing, full of energy, and action-oriented. You look for excitement, fun, pleasure, and wealth. You tend to be an uptight person who explodes easily into anger.

You are a seeker of the pleasurable things in life, and you could lose your independence through addiction to alcohol, drugs, sex, food—all that money can buy. You can become addicted to the excitement of doing daring, high-risk things. By being independent and doing your own thing, you could become captured by the things you seek.

In your friendship and love relationships you tend to be very forceful and to use people up and move on.

At your best, you have great leadership ability, and you are willing to take on challenges that most people would rather pass up. You are the kind of person who can walk into the lion's den and tame the beasts.

You can be a very valuable and much admired person in society, but if you don't have respect for others you could become a very dangerous person. Breaking the rules or "striking fear in the hearts of people" could be fun for you, but if you get carried away with doing this, if you push too hard, if you do too much to people, their fear turns into anger, and anger can turn into violence against you.

At your worst, you could become ruthless, violent, and destructive. Instead of taming the beasts, you could become one of them. At your best, you could be a giver of life; at your worst, you could be a taker of life.

You need to become more of a people lover, or you will find yourself without friends and with many enemies. For your own good, as well as the good of others, you need to show people that you are kind and loving. If you let arrogance and greed get hold of you, you will become a dangerous person.

The other type of Chief:

THE STATESMAN

A statesman is a wise political leader. You have a quiet strength and power. You are not easily upset. By the force of your personality you are able to bring quarreling people together and get them to cooperate with each other.

You go on the attack only when family and friends are in some way threatened. You are slow to anger but when it comes you take charge of things, and no one with any sense questions your authority.

At your best, you are strong willed and mild mannered. You feel close to both children and nature. You do not experience the anxieties, fears, and insecurities that most people do. You tend to have two faces. In public, you are outgoing and forceful; in private, you are gentle and relaxed.

You are attracted to a spirituality that seeks the invisible Source of power through nature. In it you find the source of your own powers.

Although you are naturally a people lover, you are still strong willed. If you let yourself get too frustrated and angry when things aren't going your way, you get numb, and your love for people disappears as you go into a blind rage and attack all the people and things you have loved and respected.

You can avoid this by learning to put a distance between your efforts to make people and things become the way you want them to be and accepting the way things are. As often as you can, "go fishing." Spend time by yourself, relaxing and enjoying the goodness and beauty that is all around you. You can get too serious, and that's not good for you.

Some Final Advice

One of the great pieces of wisdom that humanity has come to learn is that the source of power is compassion: kind, caring, and forgiving love. Compassion can be twisted and turned into cruel vengeance through selfishness, arrogance, and hate.

Evil does not have a separate power source from good. The human mind and the human will can, and often does, take the power of goodness that all humans possess and turn it into destructive energy. Evil is good turned inside out.

Your great gift is the ability to make others feel safe and secure, and people naturally want to be loyal to you in return.

Respect this gift, and use it well.

TYPE 9

the *Peacemaker*

General Description

If you are truly a Peacemaker, you probably remember your early childhood as being peaceful, easygoing, and happy. You would like it to be that way again. This may or may not have been the actual reality, but you like to remember it that way. You looked up to your parents or guardians, and somehow you felt that you knew how they wanted you to be. You went along with it; this was okay with you. You were not inclined to cut your own path. You very much wanted your folks and family to get along. If and when they quarreled, you just got out of the way until the thunderstorm passed.

Tranquility is your focus. What you want most is a peaceful, contented, hassle-free life: a world where everyone gets along well with each other, and no one tries to force anyone to do anything.

To make this world happen, and to keep it peaceful, you want to get along well with others so that you won't upset them and they won't upset you. You want to be gentle and cooperative, and you are very willing to postpone your own wants and needs to keep life simple and uncomplicated.

In the back of your mind you know that this is a very difficult way to be—pleasing others, ignoring yourself. People often take your easygoing nature for granted. They take for granted that you will automatically go along with being the way they want you to be, that you will easily go along with whatever they want.

People don't know how angry you are inside because of this. You even try to tell yourself that you are not angry. You feel anger as a frightening, hostile experience. You don't like to feel it in yourself or feel it coming from others. It's not that you are a coward. It's just that you don't want anger and hostility in your world.

Because there *is* anger and hostility, you have learned to withdraw into the world of nature or into the world of your imagination. Here you find the beauty and peacefulness that you enjoy so much. You also enjoy children. Children don't seem to be aware of all the nasty realities of life, and you enjoy their innocence, openness, and the joy they have in just being themselves. They can be happy and playful even in very difficult surroundings.

You conceal your anger from others and yourself very well until someone directly, openly tells you to do something that you don't want to do; then you can get very upset:

"I need to be happy with the way things are and I try so hard to be cooperative and generous. Now here is someone ordering me around. This has gone too far. I refuse to cooperate. I won't do it and no one can make me. People don't understand how hard I try to go along with their wishes. I have my own needs and wants. Why won't other people cooperate with me the way I cooperate with them? I have my rights too! I like things the way they are (were). Why don't people leave me alone?"

After you explode in anger, you regret what you did. You destroyed the peaceful world. You apologize to others, and you put yourself down.

When others have pushed you around long enough, you tend to get paranoid—fearful and suspicious of other people's intentions. Your imagination can carry you into experiencing the world as a hostile, threatening place in which you constantly have to protect yourself. You may try to be a "tough guy," and force others to be the way you want them to be or get deeply into the search for a child-like, hassle-free world, where there are no problems, where you don't have to do anything to please others, where you don't have to make any decisions for yourself.

When you were younger—and maybe still—you would go along with whatever your friends were doing just because you wanted to be a part of their lives. The Peacemaker characteristically does not feel the need to assert his or her individuality. The Peacemaker is more likely to become attached to someone else who does have this drive and to "go along for the ride."

When big changes start happening in your life you can become helpless, neglectful, and irresponsible, stubbornly refusing to take any initiative, unable to make decisions, unable to do the things that you need to do to grow into a self-reliant and independent person. When you become like this, you may even unconsciously torpedo your own efforts at independence.

Under the constant pressure from others to "make something of yourself," you can become preoccupied with doing all sorts of unnecessary things as you keep trying to figure out what to do that will make others get off your back. You can become fixated on one solution: a person, a career, a job, a place of residence that will solve everything. In doing so, you are not asking yourself "what is good for me?" You are asking "what will make others happy with me so that life will be peaceful?"

Because you are not choosing something that fits your own goodness, talents, and natural skills, what you decide will not likely be good for you. When others say "do something with your life," what you are inclined to hear them saying is "Become the way I want you to be." If they really love you and care for you, what they are actually saying is, "do whatever it is that you need to do to become independent, productive, and strong. Do it in the way that you feel is best for you; but just do it. When you do this you will become happy and contented with yourself. When you become happy and contented with your own separate identity, you will become peaceful with yourself and the world, and you will discover your inherent goodness."

When you are at your best you have a comfortable inner strength and a child-like quality about you that makes you very endearing and lovable. When you are at your worst, your strength and childlikeness becomes weakness and childishness. You become very dependent on others to make things better for you.

Some Advice

Personal growth and development, becoming an independent, productive, and strong person are hard. Making your own decisions can be difficult because you can't make everybody happy. Remember that not making your own personal growth decisions and following through on them will make everybody unhappy, and you will not be able to achieve the contented, peaceful world that you so much desire.

A Peacemaker does not like changes. It is hard to be peaceful and contented in the present situation, and change means having to start all over again. Realistically, by the time you were ten years old, the world stopped being a natural, automatic, "given" world. The world keeps changing, and no matter how you may try to avoid it, you keep changing too. Through careful, realistic planning, hard work, decision making, and the right kind of stubbornness (in pursuing personal goals), you will discover that in the doing of this you will become peaceful and contented.

Happiness is not a life situation in the past that you need to regain. Happiness is found in doing the things that you need to do to make that happy life become a reality. This means changing with your age, changing as your world changes.

At your best you are a tremendous lover of people and nature. Unfortunately, when you are not at your best you can be very difficult to live with. You tend to blame others for the problems that you are having. It is not other people's fault for the way you are. It's not your "fault" either if, knowing the way you are, you are struggling, learning to assert yourself by taking a one-step-at-a-time, realistic approach to your personal development. Be careful not to blame those you love. You are where you are as a result of personal decisions you have made (not to decide is a decision, going along with what you think other people want is also a decision).

Keep your loved ones posted on how you are feeling day by day. Don't assume that they will always understand or that they will agree with you. Ask for their opinions, but don't take these opinions as "orders" that you have to agree with. Take their opinions as suggestions. This leaves you free to agree or disagree. And if you disagree, be aware of your tendency to then say "it's your fault that I disagree." Especially in a love relationship, it is important to learn how to agree to disagree—without feeling guilty about your anger.

No matter how hard two lovers may try, the two worlds never fully become one. The best world for lovers to live in is a world where two worlds can lovingly coexist.

During the times when you realize that you have made decisions that were wrong for you, write them down. Don't forget the insight. Ask yourself how you could have decided differently. Learn from the mistake by turning it into a learning experience. Remember, so that when the same or a similar situation comes again, you will decide in a better way. Blaming solves nothing. Learning solves a lot.

Your hidden strength is the patient pursuit of doing good, realistic, and worthwhile things. You may not realize this, but it's true. You are not accustomed to seeing yourself as an individual person. You also want very much to be united with a strong, "go for it" individual. Imagine yourself as this kind of individual and unite with this image, fall deeply in love with it. Merge with it, and you will become this person.

Understanding what you need to do is not the same thing as getting it done. When decision time comes for you, research the many possibilities. Set a time limit on this research because you have a strong tendency to analyze things to death.

Weigh the pros and cons of each possibility, and ask others to help you with this. You tend to think the worst or only the best of each option. Discussing these options with another person is a good and needed reality check for you. Set a time limit for this and stick to it.

Then make your decision on your own. Don't decide against something because someone recommended it. Don't decide for something because you want to please someone else. Knowing your natural interests and talents, decide on what is best for you.

In making your decisions, be aware of your tendency to fear change. Be aware of your great sensitivity to what others might think of your decision. Be aware that there is no such thing as a final solution. Be aware of your tendency to redecide past decisions. Every decision you make creates the need for further decisions; this is normal. Backtracking makes life very confusing and frustrating. With rare exception, having gone through the careful decision-making process, it is best to say, "Here is where I find myself as a result of past decisions. What new decisions do I need to make to move things forward?" Don't go back on decisions that you have made. Do your best to work through difficulties.

The Two Paths

TOWARD HEALTH AND GROWTH

Work to become self-assured, inner-directed, and very active in self-development and personal growth activities. Try to become flexible and independent, able to use anger to get yourself to do good and worthwhile things for yourself and others. A healthy Nine is peaceful because he or she is no longer afraid of anger or of change. Knowing how to use the energy of anger to do the things you need to do to stand on your own is a skill you need to learn. Try to see change as a sign of life, not death.

WARNING (Signs of trouble)

Avoid becoming too easygoing, becoming a follower, pretending your problems are not serious, developing a born-to-lose attitude. Beware of avoiding doing what you know you need to do to stand on your own. Notice when you are letting your feelings become overly sensitive to what others might be thinking—becoming angry when others try to get you to do the things that you need to do. If surprising outbursts of anger start happening, take this as a sign that you need to make some changes in yourself.

TOWARD UNHEALTH AND BREAKDOWN

If you have delayed in doing what you need to do, you fall behind in personal growth, and you blame others for it or you get very down on yourself and find ways to punish yourself. You begin to fear that you can't handle the serious side of life. You panic, become cowardly, and run when people try to get you to do necessary things. You get into drugs, alcohol, or easy sex to numb these fears. When you get intoxicated, you stop being nice and easygoing and become abusive and very violent.

GROWTH STEPS

Become a doer of good things that will make you an independent, self-reliant, "doing just fine on my own" kind of person—breaking attachments to family, friends, and home until you can do this. Make your own "place in the sun."

When you can make it on your own, you will find that those who love you will love you all the more. If they don't, find new friends who will respect you and be loyal to you.

Now you will find the fun, happiness, and peace that you seek; respected, secure and safe in yourself, loving and helping others. You always had it in you to be a tremendous lover. Now you can do it, and do it very well.

Your Spirituality

There are many kinds of spirituality. The kind that may be best for you has to do with your love of nature and animals and with your desire to be united with someone greater than yourself.

By noticing, studying, and appreciating the beauty of nature, you are likely to discover your path to the Higher Power, the Creator, the Person that you will be able to unite with more closely than with any human being.

If you come from a spiritual background that believes that everything that exists has some kind of life, some kind of spirit, and if you believe that death is just a change from flesh and spirit to just spirit, you are probably aware of realities that other people are not.

If this is true for you,

1. Know that you are not "some kind of crazy" for experiencing things that others do not experience.
2. Don't be afraid of these experiences. The unknown, the unusual are not in themselves dangerous.

3. Avoid becoming hooked on these experiences. They may help you in your growth, but you could use them to avoid doing the practical, ordinary things that you need to do.

4. Seek out a spiritual adviser-companion who is experienced in these matters. Find someone who is comfortable with your experiences. Listen to the advice that is given, then make up your own mind.

5. Seriously consider the understanding that along with the ones you love most in this world, the Creator of all is the one you need to relate to most. All other spiritual realities are meant to help you and others to become better people and are meant to help you seek and find this greatest relationship of all.

6. Get to know and appreciate your own natural goodness. Experiencing your own goodness is the stepping stone to any spirituality that is worthy of your time and interest.

Fine Tuning

There are two types of Peacemakers:

THE PERSON-ORIENTED NINE

You have two sides to you that don't work well together. One side is a people lover who is charming, warm, loving, patient, and calm although somewhat lazy. The other side (the side that you don't like to think about) can be very pushy, angry, possessive, jealous, and violent.

You are very focused on people, especially your family and close friends, and you want them to get along well. You try to make this happen through a fun-loving, joking manner, but when this doesn't work you can become very angry, forceful, punishing, and physically violent against the very people you love most. When this happens, you quickly regret what you did because of your trigger temper.

As a result of your anger toward them and anger toward yourself for losing self-control, you may cut yourself off from those you love and seek the company of other more cheerful and easygoing people. You tend to make believe that the outburst never happened.

You have strong sexual urges that you give in to easily. You are very possessive and jealous of your lover—you claim exclusive rights over him or her, and you defend these rights.

However, you feel free to play the field once in a while when the urge to do so comes over you. You don't see this as a betrayal because your "extracurricular activities" are one-nighters.

Just as you can be abusive to those you love, you can also be abusive toward yourself by putting yourself in dangerous situations with alcohol and drug abuse or careless sex through which you try to numb the conflicts within you. You also can be self-defeating—torpedoing your own efforts at personal development by causing failure when you are on the verge of success.

It is very important for you to notice and accept both sides of yourself. Don't divide yourself up by pretending you have only one side. Accept the fact that you can't change other people. If people don't want to change, accept them the way they are or move on.

You need to work on self-control. Start first with physical control. Start with small things that you need to do every day, then work on your behavior toward others.

Accept that independence and self-reliance will take long, disciplined, and hard work. Don't be afraid to succeed; it will make you even more lovable.

The other type of Peacemaker:

THE REFORMER NINE

All the things that have been said about the Peacemaker are true for you except that you are quieter than the other type of Nine, and you "stuff" your feelings more. You are more self-controlled because you are idealistic and have high principles for yourself. You want to be a moral leader for others, and you want to do it through the way you live and behave. You don't have the intense inner conflict that your partner Nine has, but you feel your conflicts more because you are more sensitive to other people's feelings and because you are much more honest with yourself.

You tend to be a conservative person, even a little strait-laced. Even though you want to avoid all personal conflicts with others, and you don't relate as easily to people as your partner Nine does, you could be a good organizer and manager of people and activities once you realize and accept the fact that you can't make everybody happy no matter how hard you try.

Your big problem is that you repress your feelings. You let your anger and anxieties eat away at you so you are vulnerable to headaches and ulcers. Although you are usually easygoing and flexible, when your anger comes out it explodes, and you can be very inflexible and intolerant.

You need to have someone to talk to who will be able to listen to your anger and frustrations about the wrong things that people do. When you let your feelings out in this conversational way you need not necessarily be looking for advice. The main purpose is to let your feelings out rather than letting them build up.

If you let yourself "stew" about problems you can get yourself into the situation where you can't think about anything else, and you can lose the larger view of things.

Some Final Advice

Anger will always be a fact of life for you. It won't go away. Get used to it, and use it. Your anger is body energy. Do regular physical exercise to let it out. Keep your weight down. Make physical fitness an important goal for yourself.

You can also use this body energy to accomplish your self-development goals. Let the energy from your gut rise up through your body into your head. This may seem a strange thing to say, but if you do it your body energy will turn into mind energy. Once you do this, you will not only be physically healthier, you will be able to accomplish anything that you set your mind to.

Index